Tails

of a Dog

Psychoanalyst

by
C. W. Meisterfeld

Illustrations
by Walt Lee

First Edition
October 1978

M-R-K- Publishing

Library of Congress Catalog Card Number
78-58-492

ISBN 0-901292-2-7

M-R-K Publishing
Rural Route Number 6
Petaluma, California 94952

Acknowledgments

To Ina Ray Scrocco. . .
Your help and guidance was greatly needed and
appreciated. Thank you for being such a beautiful
Sagittarian.

To my friend, who wished to remain anonymous. . .
Your constructive criticism was very helpful.
(Now I know what "yami'yami" is!) **Dankeschön.**

To Jack, Gladys, Claude and Gina. . .
My gratitude for sharing your personal experiences.

To Charlotte J. Schriber. . .
Your hours, weeks and months of dedication,
selflessness and wisdom, far exceeded my expectations.
May you be blessed such as I.

Introduction

What is a dog psychoanalyst? That seems to be the question most people ask me. Essentially, psychoanalyzing a dog is similar to psychoanalyzing a human being. It is a method of treating neurosis and other mental disorders by analyzing emotional conflicts, repressions, etc. The difference, of course, is that dogs cannot verbalize what is troubling them.

In 1964, when I began to specialize in dog behavioral problems and neurosis, the subject was not as widely recognized as it is today. Therefore the concepts and methods described throughout this book have been gleaned from my own experiences in working with the problems of dogs and their owners.

The following stories are all true; only some of the names have been changed to protect the innocent. (Dogs, that is!) For a different perspective, several stories were written by the clients themselves (their names are real).

Inasmuch as these stories are approached from my standpoint as a professional trainer and dog psychoanalyst, and from the standpoint of some of my clients, I felt it was only fair to include some stories from the dog's standpoint as well. Since Ming, Duchess and Leroy were unable to recount their experiences, I have written their stories for them. However these stories are also true, and the fact that I wrote them should not detract from their authenticity to any great extent.

I could go on about my work, philosophy, and beliefs, but I have resolved to keep this introduction short and let the stories speak for themselves. If you, the reader, have been informed, enlightened, or entertained, I, as an author, could not ask for more.

C. W. Meister

Also author of *How's & Why's of Psychological Dog Training**

*Published by M-R-K Publishing

Table of Contents

Leaving It All Behind

Wintertime. I sat gazing through my livingroom window at the ice jamming up in the Vermillion River. The sight always fascinated me. One moment the river appears to be asleep under a solid blanket of ice; and if you don't recognize the banks, the river looks just like open fields or meadows. Suddenly there is a loud crunching sound, then silence. A few minutes later more crunching and grinding sounds penetrate the cold air. All at once several giant slabs of ice rear up toward the sky. They seem almost alive, struggling to free themselves, to "return from whence they came."

The jangling of the telephone broke my reverie, and I got up to answer it.

"Hello, this Bill Meisterfeld?"

"Yes, who's calling?"

"This is Al Johnson from California."

"California?"

"Owner of Johnson's Boarding Kennel. You stopped by last month to talk with me, remember?"

"Right, yes. I remember now. How are you?"

"Fine, fine. Say, I read those newspaper articles you left me; quite impressive. If you are still interested in re-establishing your training kennel, we might be able to work something out."

Now *that* was the main reason my friend Ray and I ventured to California. We both wanted to relocate and get away from the winter dreariness of Ohio, so we spent two weeks touring the "Sunny State." We received precious little encouragement to stay however, as good job prospects were hard to find. I got the feeling that Californians weren't all that anxious to receive winter refugees from the East. I had even heard horror stories about people stopping at the border for inspection, and if it looked like they were trying to move to California,

9

the border officials turning them around and sending them back home. It probably wasn't true, but the thought made me shudder just the same.

Toward the end of our trip I had resigned myself to the fact that I would probably be stuck in Ohio for the rest of my life. It was just by chance that we passed "Johnson's Boarding Kennel" while driving through beautiful Marin County. Ray encouraged me to go in and talk to the owner about working there as a trainer. "What have you got to lose?" he argued. So I did. Al Johnson was a pleasant man and listened to my proposal with mild interest. I left some newspaper write-ups on my dog Baroness and myself, and then, with Ray, headed back to Ohio. I didn't expect anything to come of it, which was why I was surprised to hear from Al.

"I'd like you to talk to a friend of mine," Al said. "His name's Phil and he's a veterinarian. Here he is."

A different voice came over the phone. "Hello, I hear you're thinking about coming out here."

"Yes, I have been considering it for some time," I said. "Wasn't sure I could swing it financially though."

"Well, I'll tell you," Phil said. "I came here to California from Iowa about five years ago. I wish I'd done it *fifteen* years ago! People here seem to be more health conscious, and they don't mind spending money on their animals for the best of care. It's a lot different than the midwest. My practice has grown fantastically here."

"No kidding. *That's* certainly encouraging."

"You bet. If you decide to come out, stop by and see my place. It's called the Fairfax Veterinary Hospital. Nice talking with you."

"Thank you, and same here."

"Al here again. What do you think? Does this sound like what you want?"

"It sure does, Al. I appreciate your offer immensely. Would you mind if I gave you my answer in a week?"

"No, not at all. You have my number?"

"Yes, I still have your business card. I'll be in touch with you."

I was excited with the anticipation of making a move as I hung up the phone. Maybe it *would* be possible after all. I wasn't getting very far staying in Ohio, that was certain. Business came to a dead halt during the winter months while my clients all hibernated. What did Phil say? He should have moved there fifteen years earlier? I called Al Johnson the next day and told him I was coming.

I had been renovating the old summer cottage that I was living in at that time, and it took me another month to complete it. It had been a kind of haven for me and I vowed after my divorce, never to leave it. This was perhaps the most difficult part of my decision to move. My cottage was high and dry, safe from Spring flooding, yet it was only fifty feet from the basement door to my private boat dock on the river where I swam, fished, snorkled, boated and trained my duck dogs. Sure loved that temperamental old river; sometimes muddy, sometimes clear, but I mustn't forget *frozen* one third of the time! I left my paradise by the river finished, furnished and unoccupied, with great hopes for a successful future. California, here I come!

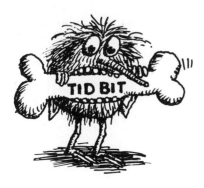

The universe is a garden; whatever one plants,
one must also someday harvest.

Fay

California was like a whole new world to me. The climate, the people, the customs were all so delightfully different. Al Johnson had planned a dinner around my interview. It was here, over a New York steak, that I first met Fay Owyung.

I was sure it was not a coincidence that we had been seated together. He was fairly short, with a pleasant Oriental face. His dark eyes regarded me keenly as our small talk turned to dogs. He began to question me on just about every facet of training and showing dogs. I didn't know anything about Fay other than his name, but it was obvious to me that he knew a great deal about dogs. His questions were precise and sometimes tricky. But I must have answered most of them correctly.

The next day I stopped by to see Al. He was in a good mood. "Hello Bill," he said smiling. "You've had a real favorable interview last night. We should get together soon to make arrangements for you to start a training school."

"That's great. I'm available any time. Thank you for all your help."

"Don't mention it, Bill."

"I sure enjoyed talking with Mr. Owyung," I ventured. "Ah, what does he do?"

"Oh Fay's a trainer." he answered nonchalantly. "Probably one of the best in California. He belongs to the Professional Handlers Association. Been in the dog business for years. I think he knows about all there is to know about breeding German Shepherds. I've seen him just look at one and tell what breed line it came from. He's one exceptional groomer too; does all breeds. Yeah, he's really into dogs in a big way that guy. That's why I asked him to help me with the interview."

Six months later, I left Marin and opened my own training and boarding kennel on the outskirts of Petaluma. Since our first meeting, I had run into Fay a couple of times in downtown Petaluma, but we seldom exchanged more than a nod and a hello. That's why I was very surprised to get a call from him one day.

"This is Fay Owyung." he greeted. "Do you have a little time to spare? I was hoping you could drop by my place. I'd like to show you something."

I asked him where he lived and how to get there. "Sure. I could be there in say half an hour?"

"Good. See you then."

I hung up the phone, puzzled. What could he want to see me about?

Fay was waiting for me as I pulled into his driveway. He smiled and greeted me like an old friend, then gave me a tour of his training kennel. He was much more relaxed and animated than he had been at our dinner. He talked easily.

"I want you to see something," he said, then disappeared into a kennel. He brought out a shifty-eyed German Shepherd and tied his leash to a post. Fay stood back and made some threatening gestures with his arms and hands. The dog bared his teeth and began to growl and lunge on the end of his leash.

"Now watch," he said as he bent down and picked up a handful of tiny pebbles. One at a time he flipped a pebble in the dog's direction, where they landed just short of him. I thought he was asking for trouble, getting this dog so riled up. Fay just stood still, staring with hawk-like eyes at the angry dog, flipping the pebbles. Then, without any words or hand signals from Fay, the dog suddenly stopped snapping and growling, and with his tail tucked up, retreated. Fay turned to me and smiled, saying nothing.

"What did you do?" I blurted out finally.

"I talked to him." He tapped his temple with his finger. "Mentally. I said, 'If you bite me, I'll bite you back!' And as you saw, it works."

"Incredible!" I found his demonstration very fascinating. Yet why was he showing this to me, his competator? Professional trainers normally guard their hard-earned techniques zealously. In this business you learn mostly by trial and error.

"Wait here." he said. "I want you to see another dog I'm working with." He returned with the biggest German Shepherd I'd ever seen. "Here Bill, let me see you put him through his paces. He knows all the commands and hand signals." He held out the leash to me.

I suddenly felt as if he were testing me the way he'd done at our first meeting. Was *this* why he asked me here? Fay noticed my hesita-

THE BIGGEST GERMAN SHEPHERD I'D EVER SEEN...

tion and looked at me quizzically. "Haven't you ever worked a Shepherd before?" he said grinning. I knew I was cornered. I sensed that he had chosen this particular dog for a reason, but what could it be?

I took hold of the leash resolutely. "Heel!" I commanded a little too loudly. I hoped my uneasiness wasn't obvious. My bluff seemed to be working, however, because the Shepherd responded well to my commands. We did some fast, normal and slow heeling. He sat quickly on abrupt halts, and dropped on the down command. I marveled at Fay's abilities and was thankful for not having to compete with him in any A.K.C. obedience trials. He would be tough to beat. I handed the dog back to him and felt that this time I should speak up and ask some questions.

"Okay, what was that all about?" Fay tried to keep from smiling.

"Excuse me a minute, I have to put this dog back."

"Fine, I'll wait." I was determined to get some answers.

When he came back he looked at me with shining eyes. "That dog you just worked? He's tough. Tougher than the first one you saw. He came after me a few times while I was training him. I had to find out if he disliked being trained, or if he disliked me personally. Now I know it was a personal thing, because he didn't try to get funny with you." I felt my knees go weak.

Driving home it dawned on me why Fay had shown me that first trick. It was his way of compensating me for playing his guinea pig. I liked Fay. I hoped one day to be able to share and compare our knowledge.

I thought maybe that day had arrived when he hailed me down in a grocery parking lot. I was just leaving when I spotted him waving. He went to his station wagon and brought out another German Shepherd. I thought he must really take me for a "Dumb Kraut" to fall for *that* one again.

"Pay me twenty dollars in advance for bandaids and I'll handle him!" I said as he strode over to me. He laughed.

"No, this dog does not have any problems, I guarantee it. Just walk him a little and give him a few commands. I want to be sure he will respond to his owner."

Oh what the hell, I thought. I don't mind taking a chance if I'm going to learn something. I took the leash and like the true showman (ham?) that I am, did some fast and fancy work with the dog. He handled even better than the last one. His movements were truly precise.

Fay then took the dog and put him back in his station wagon and rolled up all the windows. He turned to me and said, "Now you rattle the door, make some noise, rap on the windows. Do anything you like."

"If this dog is trained to burst through windows, I'm getting out of here," I said joking.

"Ah come on. Just try it. You're safe, I promise."

I shrugged by shoulders and decided to humor him. First a little rattle on the door handle. Then a wee rap on the glass. The dog lay on the back seat looking for the most part bored to death. I rattled harder and rapped louder but the dog didn't move. I thought he was going to start snoring any minute. I went around to the side window and with arms spread and fingers outstretched, I bared my teeth and growled menacingly. The only response I provoked was from a curious passerby.

I was about to comment on what a pussycat he was, when Fay made an almost inaudible sound. Instantly that lethargic "pussycat" came to life, transformed into a snarling, snapping rage. He would have torn me to pieces if he had been able to get to me. Fay uttered another command and the dog retreated immediately. He didn't even try to squeeze in an extra growl. He lay back down and looked just like he had before. Fay walked up to me. "Well, what do you think?"

I realized that I had been standing there with my mouth open. "I think your ability as a protection dog trainer is outstanding. Superb!" I narrowed my eyes at him. "And so is your ability to confound me." We laughed.

I've always admired Fay Owyung's vast knowledge and seemingly unlimited talents. I regret never having asked him while he was alive just how he had trained that dog to such perfection. It was a demonstration I will never forget.

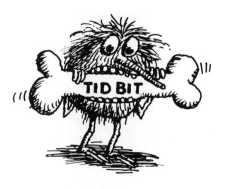

Anyone can be a good trainer; for it is not based on outer circumstances, but on our mental attitude, which is vibrated to our dogs, and on being sensitive to their needs and responses.

The Winner

The idea came to me one day shortly after I'd moved to California. I was sitting in Barney's Tavern sipping a glass of beer, and several patrons were tossing dice for drinks. Then it struck me. I stood up and cleared my throat.

"If anyone here can round up three or four dogs, I'll bet this gentleman," I motioned toward Barney, the tavern owner, "that I can make them all sit and stay for two minutes. If I can, the drinks will be on the house. If I can't, the drinks will be on me." I paused. "Is it a bet?"

The other patrons looked expectantly at the owner. He eyed me thoughtfully. "It's a bet," he said finally. There was a general rush for the door as several gentlemen set out on an impromptu dog hunt. Californians certainly are a sporting bunch, I thought.

It wasn't long before one fellow returned with a confused-looking mongrel tucked under his arm. The man was panting and covered with sweat, but obviously pleased with himself.

"Bring him right over here," I said. I took the dog and positioned him to face me with his back close to a wall. I turned and addressed Barney.

"I'd like to request that two corrections be allowed for each dog; if I don't produce by the third try, you win." Barney nodded his agreement. I turned my attention back to the dog, who I'm sure was wondering how he'd gotten himself into this. I held his muzzle gently with my right hand and forced him to look at me. "Stay," I said, staring into his eyes while I held my left palm in front of his face. I repeated the stay command and relaxed my hold on his muzzle. The dog gazed back at me intently. I continued to repeat the command, flashing my left palm in front of his face as I stared at him. The dog remained seated.

About that time another man burst in, holding his trousers up with one hand. The other hand gripped his belt which was looped

19

around the neck of a reluctant Doberman Pincer. He dragged the dog, nails scraping across the floor, to where I was. I went through the same procedure as I had with the first dog, though the Doberman proved to be more uncooperative. I finally managed to get him to sit.

The next three dogs came in all at once. One by one, I lined them up and made them sit, often going back to the first ones to reinforce the command. I must have looked like a circus performer who spun plates on the ends of those long sticks. One plate starts to wobble and he has to run back to start it again until he has them all spinning at the same time. The Doberman broke twice, making it necessary for me to correct him. Once more and I'd be buying a whole lot of drinks.

Finally I managed to get them all sitting at the same time. I stood in front of them with my left hand up, repeating firmly but softly, "Stay, stay, stay." The Doberman made a move to stand up. "Stay!" I said gruffly, and glared into his eyes. He checked himself, much to my relief.

Another half minute to go. The dogs eyes were all fixed on me. If they started to look away, I would repeat the command to bring their attention back to me. Two minutes.

Suddenly the tavern filled with laughter and congratulations. And why not? Everyone had a free drink, and I was a hero. The dogs all scampered out the door and I sat down to enjoy my victory.

I had learned long ago how to establish my dominance over a dog through the use of my eyes. The secret to using this method with dogs is to project feelings of strength and supremacy *without* presenting yourself as a challenge to them. A dog who feels challenged may react fearfully or resort to aggression. So, as I'm staring into the dog's eyes, he senses that I am not a threat or a challenge to him, only that I am in command of him. I establish myself as number one, and the dog is more willing to obey me. The greatest advantage to this is that it looks dramatic.

Up until that time in the tavern, I'd never attempted this trick in public. I suppose it was a mixture of the gambler and ham in me that gave me the idea. In any case, my ego was sufficiently fortified for me to perform the same feat in other taverns throughout the area.

Once in a while, I would add a daring twist by using a dog that belonged to the proprieter of the establishment, or to one of the patrons. In this case I would let the owner of the dog try and coax it to break the sit-stay command. One determined tavern owner even used a piece of ham to try and persuade his eight-year-old Schnauzer to break. In spite of temptation, the dog held his stay—much to his owner's chagrin. I never thought much about the possibility of losing. My success had given me a sense of cocky self-assuredness. I suppose I was ripe for a defeat.

It happened one afternoon at Dinucci's, a restuarant-tavern in Valley Ford. It was fairly quiet that day. Only a handful of people were scattered about the room, so I decided to liven things up a bit. I realized the chances of finding any stray dogs were slim because the population of Valley Ford, at that time, was only about a hundred people, and the next town of Bodega Bay was ten miles away. But I announced my challenge anyway.

"I got a dog in my pick-up." The voice belonged to a tall, slim man sitting alone. He was obviously a rancher by the way he was dressed; cowboy hat, blue jeans, boots.

"Great! Do you agree to the terms?"

"Yep, sounds okay to me."

"Fine," I said, warming to the man. "Why don't you just bring your dog right in, Mr. uh. . ."

"Bruhn. Les Bruhn."

"Mr. Bruhn, and we'll get started." As he went outside to get his dog, I wondered what type of drink I was going to order after I'd won.

Les came back with a Border Collie heeling at his feet. "His name's Boy," he said.

"Nice-looking dog," I replied. "I'll just take him over there." I reached down to take hold of the dog's collar and stopped cold. Boy regarded me with an icy-calm stare that seemed to go right through me. I knew right then that I was sunk. I had never before (or since) seen such strong eyes in a dog. But, a bet's a bet.

I led the dog over to a far corner and sat him down facing me. He was extremely cooperative and my hopes began to rise. Maybe I could win after all. I held up my left palm and bumped him lightly on the nose several times while repeating the stay command over and over. I poured out all my mental strength as I stared into his eyes. Boy stared right back at me with equal intensity. He complied, but I had the uneasy feeling that he was just humoring me. I hoped I was wrong.

I walked back to Les, keeping an eye on the dog. "Okay," I said, sounding a lot more confident than I felt. "Try and get him up."

Les smiled and snapped his fingers. Before I could even open my mouth, Boy was sitting at his feet. I was stunned.

Les was very gentlemanly about it and gave me four extra tries. I could have been given four *hundred* tries, for when Boy heard his

master's signal, there was no stopping him.

"What is it about your dog?" I asked after the house had been set up. "I mean, his eyes are so strong. I've never seen anything like it."

"That's characteristic of a good Border Collie," he explained. "They concentrate the power of their eyes to hold the sheep in a certain spot, and keep them from moving." He nodded toward his dog. "Boy here is one of the best."

Beaten at my own game, by a dog who knew just as much about it as I did! Well, I guess it was inevitable. However, I'm glad I met my defeat at the hands of Les Bruhn and his dog. Les and I have remained friends since that first meeting, but that was the last time I ever performed my trick. I'd probably never run into another dog like Boy, but why chance it?

Demetrius

I hung up the phone and wondered whether I should have agreed to the consultation. I had never before worked a dog that couldn't walk.

"I had him checked out by my vet and two specialists from Davis, one a neurologist, and they all came up with the same diagnosis—it's psychosomatic," Dr. Renault explained over the phone. "They couldn't find any physical reason for these . . . spells. I saw in your ad that you do psychological training, so I thought you might be able to help."

"Well, this is a new one on me," I said, "but if you bring him up I'll be glad to take a look at him."

"Fine. Would 11:00 be all right?"

"This morning?"

"Yes, I have to do *something* for him as soon as possible. I'm really at a loss."

"Okay, then. I'll see you at 11:00."

As I reflected on our conversation, I began to have some doubts. I had only been specializing in problem and neurotic dogs for a few years and had begun the delicate process of building a favorable reputation for myself in this new field. Had I bitten off too much this time? I pondered the possible causes for such behavior in a dog. It was no use. I'd just have to wait and see the dog. It would take him at least an hour and a half from San Francisco; in the meantime, I busied myself with training.

The car pulled into the parking lot and stopped. A distinguished looking man got out of the driver's side, opened the rear car door, and took hold of a leash. He gave it a couple of tugs and out popped a Dalmation like a cork. I watched as the dog took four or five steps and collapsed to the ground. I went out to meet the doctor.

"I hope I'm at the right place. Are you Mr. Meisterfeld?"

"Yes, and yes," I answered, offering my hand. "Why don't you bring him inside?" I stepped back to see how Dr. Renault was going to accomplish this.

"Let's go, Demetrius," he said, smacking his lips several times. He gave a couple tugs on the leash, but the limp dog regarded him passively and made no move to get up. Finally Dr. Renault bent down, picked him up and carried him into the office.

After depositing the dog on the carpet, Dr. Renault sat down wearily. It was clear that his concern for the dog had drained him. "What do you think?" he asked. He certainly didn't mince words.

"I think we need to talk some more," I said cautiously. "How old is he?"

"Eight months."

"And how long have you owned him?"

"Since he was about seven weeks old. We bought him from a very well known breeder in San Jose."

"Did you have a chance to see the sire and dam?"

"Fortunately, yes. They're both perfectly normal—champions, as a matter of fact. Mr. Fredrick, the breeder, showed me all the ribbons and trophies they'd won for obedience and confirmation. Oh, and they both earned their C.D.X.* too. That's what's so confusing to me; with that kind of background, why is Demetrius so messed up?"

"And clinically they couldn't find *anything* wrong?"

"No." Dr. Renault looked at me expectantly.

I wished I had something, *anything*, to tell him. What I needed was time to think. "I believe I'd like some coffee. Would you care for some, Dr. Renault?"

"No, thank you."

I went into the next room and fixed myself a cup of coffee while my mind raced for a clue to Demetrius' behavior. It would have been nice to produce a book and look up "psychosomatic illness in dogs;" but at that time (1967), the field of dog psychology and neurosis was in its infancy. I had only my experience to fall back on, which was of little help in this case. I'd never encountered anything this serious before. I did, however, have some facts, and through the process of elimination I was confident that I could at least conclude where the problem originated. If Demetrius was clinically sound, and his breeding was also sound, then the problem had to be environmental. With that, I took my coffee and rejoined Dr. Renault in the office.

"Have you done any training with him, Dr. Renault?" I asked.

"Oh, I took him to classes until he started with these spells. The

*Companion Dog Excellent

DR. RENAULT BENT DOWN, AND PICKED HIM UP...

instructor told me to drag him so that he'd be forced to walk. It didn't work, so I picked him up, carried him out and never went back. That suited my wife because she didn't want him trained anyway."

"When does he refuse to walk?"

"It varies. Sometimes when I pick up the leash he's right there, raring to go. Other times he shows absolutely no interest at all. In that case he will either refuse to walk or he will collapse later as we're walking. Then, of course, I have to carry him home. Also, at times he forgets his housebreaking. My wife gets livid if I reprimand him. We haven't had so many disagreements since our children were small."

I suspected there was something more to the situation, but further conversation did not disclose anything concrete. "Well, Dr. Renault," I said at last, "all I can promise is that I'll do my best. As long as I can see that he's making progress I'll continue with his training."

"That's fair enough," he said, and completed the arrangements for the dog's training.

When I was ready to put Demetrius in his run, I took the leash and gave him a couple pats on top of his head. With some encouraging words I started to walk out of the office, hoping he would follow me. He didn't. Demetrius was not tense or fearful, just limp as a dishrag. With as much grace as I could muster, I picked him up and carried him to his run.

After the Doctor left, I went to a peephole (built into the wall in order to view the dogs on the other side) and observed Demetrius. He lay right where I'd left him. About five minutes later he raised his head and looked around curiously; then, unaware someone was watching, he got up and walked to his outside run. I hurried outside and, hidden by some grape vines, I watched him. Demetrius walked back and forth effortlessly, with no sign of his former disability.

The first week I had no training sessions with Demetrius, although I'd visit and talk to him for a few minutes several times a day. As the days passed, he began to show some desire for me to take him out, and at the beginning of the second week, I felt he was ready for some training.

I put a leash and collar on him and led him to the ring. So far so good. I decided to put him through some of the basics to find out how much he knew. I walked him a short distance and had him sit—at least I *tried* to have him sit. When his hindquarters went down he would begin to slide sideways. I tried propping him against a wall but he still slid right or left. Finally, I sat him in a corner with his back braced against the two adjoining walls. Dr. Renault had forgotten to tell me about this problem.

With a little coaxing, I was able to start walking him around the ring. After we'd gone around once, I began to feel there was some hope for the dog. Demetrius continued walking and I was more elated as we began our second time around. I'll have him in shape in no time, I thought. Then my left hand jerked abruptly. I looked down at Demetrius sprawled on the floor—a dead weight. No amount of coaxing would get him up this time. I bent down and began to test his legs for any sign of pain reactions by pinching the flesh. Demetrius flinched so I knew that he definitely had feeling in his legs. There was nothing left to do but carry him back to his run.

I felt discouraged after my short-lived "victory," so I surrendered to the need for a break. I took a walk down by the pond to try and sort out my thoughts. As I gazed at the rippling water and breathed the fragrant air, I decided a different approach to the situation was in order. I was going to have to watch Demetrius like a hawk and catch him before he staged his act. I also resolved that this was the *last* time I was going to carry him. The only question was, what to do if he quit in the training ring again? If I just left him there I wouldn't be able to train my other dogs until he decided to get up. But what if I worked him right in his run? That way when he pulls his act, I could just leave him. Perfect!

The next morning after the runs were washed down, I began Demetrius' training session. We walked the twenty-foot-long run about five times while I was very careful not to pull on the leash. I was not about to justify his refusal to walk. I studied his every movement as my response had to be timed perfectly. As I had expected, Demetrius began to go limp as we walked. Before he had a chance to drop, I let go of the leash and it fell to the cement. Then I just walked out of the run. As I turned around to lock the gate, I glanced quickly at Demetrius, and was pleased to see a bewildered expression on his face as he tottered there. For an instant he wasn't sure if he should collapse or not. Apparently decided, he fell, and I walked away.

The next session I had with Demetrius, I introduced him to my liverwurst treats. We walked back and forth in his run several times and then I had him sit. The bottom half of the runs are built with concrete blocks, and the top half is fencing. I sat him in a corner where the concrete walls gave him support. Just as he'd start to fold, I dangled a piece of liverwurst a few inches from his nose. In response, he sat up to reach the meat. I knew he could not operate on two emotions at the same time. I used the same method when walking him. Anytime it looked like he was going to lag, I'd hold the liverwurst in front of him as we walked to entice him to keep up. I worked him for five minutes that time without him collapsing once; then I dropped the leash and walked out.

Demetrius followed me to the gate and watched as I locked it. I took out another piece of liverwurst and held it through the fence about two feet above his head. Demetrius hesitated at first, but then he stood up on his hind legs, planted his front paws against the fence and took the treat. It's very important when working a problem dog to always quit while winning, and while he is still eager to work.

When Demetrius appeared weak and didn't want to work, I cut his sessions down to two minutes. Later on in the week I was able to increase the time to eight or nine minutes. Finally he was ready to get back in the training ring.

By planning his training sessions meticulously, Demetrius made steady progress from then on. After developing his powers of concentration, we advanced through all the other exercises and commands including hand signals. In the last ten weeks, Demetrius was a willing and eager student, showing no signs of reverting to his former negative habits.

The time eventually came when Demetrius was ready for the first training session with his owners. When Dr. and Mrs. Renault arrived, I ushered them into my office and closed the door. I pulled the window curtains and turned on the radio to drown any sound they might make. I wanted to demonstrate what their dog could do before they made any contact with him. I knew that once he learned they were there, he'd be too excited to perform the best he could.

Demetrius gave a magnificant performance. The couple watched intently as I put him through all the exercises using verbal and non-verbal commands, and off-leash work as well. When I was through, I led Demetrius into the office to reunite him with his owners. It was hard to tell who was more excited, the people or the dog.

"Okay, folks, I suggest we get started with the training session before Demetrius gets too worked up emotionally. I want to avoid any possible setbacks." I explained the procedure to them, then turned the leash over to the doctor. "Any questions before you start?"

"Yes, do I praise him when he does something right?"

"Not for now. He would probably become too emotional. In the beginning, I'd suggest using your praise sparingly, if at all. And be sure to correct him *gently*. We don't want to turn him off, or you might end up having to carry him through the exercises." We laughed, but I noticed Mrs. Renault had a dubious look on her face.

Dr. Renault followed my instructions well, and soon Demetrius was working proudly for him. "That was wonderful for your first session," I remarked. "Now we'll let your wife have a go."

Dr. Renault turned the leash over to his wife and she took it hesitantly. I thought she might be a bit nervous about working him. "Do you have any questions?" I asked. She shook her head solemnly. "All right, forward."

Mrs. Renault's session was a disaster from the start. She neglected to give the heel command before stepping off, despite my repeated reminders. Worse yet, she consistently got her verbal and hand signals mixed up. After only ten minutes of working him, Demetrius was thoroughly confused and out of control. I called a halt, hoping it would give her a chance to pull herself together.

"I don't see why I have to go through all this," she said, flustered. "I don't believe in turning dogs into robots."

Dr. Renault came to my rescue. "Vivian, I *like* the way Demetrius has changed. Look at him. He's proud and happy, *and he walks.* Isn't that better than the jellyfish he was?"

"So now that he's cured, why should he have to go through all this? I'm sorry, but I just can't see it. I've had enough." With that, she walked out of the kennel.

Dr. Renault sighed dejectedly. "I was afraid of this. I was hoping that once she saw how beneficial this has been, she would accept it. I can't understand why she's against having a trained dog."

"I'm afraid I can't help you in that department," I said. "But I think you're going to have to work something out for Demetrius' sake."

"Yes, I know. I'll have a talk with my wife and I'll come up with something by next Thursday."

"Good. I'll see you then."

Come Thursday, Dr. Renault arrived promptly for his second session—alone. "Well, we've worked it out," he said cheerily, as he came inside.

"Wonderful!"

"Yep, I told Vivian that since it's my dog, I will do all the handling and so on. And she went along with it. I'm even going to build a kennel for him."

"Well, that sounds like a workable arrangement. Why don't we get started then?"

Dr. Renault continued to progress with Demetrius through the rest of his training sessions. The change in his dog was quite remarkable. By the last session he was doing off-leash work, using hand signals only.

"Do you suppose I would be able to show him?" he asked, before taking Demetrius home.

"I think he's just about ready for anything," I said. "He's come a long way and I see no reason why you shouldn't be able to show him. Why, I think he'd even give his parents a run for their money."

"Thanks, Bill. I'm very proud of him."

"Be sure and give me a call after the dog show. I'd like to know how well he did."

"Will do."

I thought a lot about Demetrius in the days following his departure; especially the first 72 hours and the first week. Those are usually the critical periods after a dog goes home in which it's most likely to revert. But since I hadn't heard from Dr. Renault, I concluded that the dog's transition went smoothly.

A little more than two weeks later I got a call from Dr. Renault. "He reverted, Bill," he said flatly.

I felt my stomach lurch. "Reverted! What happened?"

"I don't know. For the first two weeks he was just perfect. Then about four days ago he had another spell. I managed to get him up for a few seconds but then he just collapsed again. This morning he defecated in the living room. I thought I'd better call you and find out what I should do."

It was truly amazing how quickly my doubts reappeared. "Why don't you bring him in right now, then I can observe his behavior." And so, Dr. Renault brought Demetrius back and carried him in, just like he had done when he first came. I asked the doctor to call me in two days.

After he drove away, I went over to where Demetrius lay and gave the bobwhite whistle. I picked up the leash and stepped off. There was no resistance as Demetrius got up and walked beside me. After a few wobbly steps, he walked quite normally and I led him to his run and put him up. Strange.

The next day I put Demetrius through his paces for a full half hour. He performed just as he did before he left and showed no signs of reverting. I could only conclude that I let him go home a little too early before. When Dr. Renault called, I made arrangements to keep Demetrius for another week to make sure he was stable before letting him go. At the end of that week Dr. Renault arrived to pick him up.

"Well, what did you find out?" he asked.

"It's got to be something in the home environment, Jim. Are you using any undue force on him?"

"No. There hasn't been any need to. I followed your instructions faithfully."

I had him work Demetrius for twenty minutes so I could watch how he handled. Everything checked out fine and Demetrius showed no signs of faltering.

"Give him an extra firm snap on the leash, Jim."

He looked at me, wide-eyed. "But. . ."

"I know, I told you not to do that, but I want to see how he reacts." The doctor obliged me and jerked on the leash. Demetrius looked surprised for a moment, but it seemed to wash right over him. "Well, he should be okay now. Why don't you keep me up to date on his progress when you get home?"

"Okay, thanks again, Bill."

Dr. Renault called me every week to tell me Demetrius was doing fine. After the sixth week I told him there was no need to call me anymore. Satisfied that Demetrius was "holding," I dismissed his case from my mind. Although it's only occasionally that a dog reverts, I usually take it personally, and I'm always relieved when everything works out.

My first call the next Monday morning was Dr. Renault. Demetrius had just gone through another spell. This time I really felt frustrated, and had to resist the urge to groan.

"Tell me what happened," I said.

"Well, he was just fine from Monday till Thursday, but when I got home Sunday night, and took him out, he started slipping back."

"You were gone then?"

"Yes. I left town Friday for a lecture."

I was beginning to see a glimmer of light. "Jim, were you on a lecture tour the last time Demetrius reverted?"

"Let me check my calendar and I'll see. Yes, as a matter of fact, I was."

"Who takes care of Demetrius when you're gone?"

"Just my . . . wife."

I didn't need to point out the implications to him. "I suggest you just leave Demetrius in his run and don't work him for a few days. Give me a call Thursday to let me know how he is. He should be all right by then."

"Okay, Bill. In the meantime, I'm going to have a talk with Vivian. You'll hear from me Thursday."

Thursday rolled around and I arranged my training schedule so that I'd be available for his call. It came that afternoon.

"Demetrius is fine," Dr. Renault said. "He worked real well this morning. I also talked to my wife about my absences. You know how she felt about the training and all. Well, it seems that when I was gone, she let him stay in the house the whole time. He was up on the furniture, in the bed, and she'd feed him whatever she had for dinner instead of his dog food."

"That must be it, Jim. He can't handle two standards of behavior.

"Indeed. I should have connected his attacks with my absence, but it just never dawned on me. I should have talked with my wife a long time ago."

"Well, don't feel discouraged, Jim. As long as Demetrius' behavior is leveling off again, there's no real harm done. But I would suggest making some different arrangements next time you leave town."

"No need to, Bill. Vivian and I have worked it out. She's a stubborn lady at times but when it comes to the final crunch, I can always count on her. She's even agreed to learning how to work Demetrius. I appreciate all your help, Bill. Demetrius has taught us a lot."

Lulu

Like Demetrius, Lulu, a nine-month-old cross-breed, couldn't cope with the conflict between her owners, Joan and Dave. Her method of mental escape, however, was different.

Joan was the disciplinarian. She would not tolerate Lulu in any part of the house other than a corner in the kitchen where her bed was. The rest of the time, Lulu spent outside.

When Joan was gone, however, Dave would encourage Lulu to join him in the other parts of the house where he even let her up on the furniture. When Joan returned and found the telltale signs of dog hair on the couch, Lulu was severely reprimanded. Joan never knew that Dave was instigating Lulu's misbehavior.

Lulu managed to hold up against this barrage of hot and cold treatment until she was about six months old. That's when she began to eliminate in the house, even though she had been housebroken since she was three months old. Joan reprimanded her for breaking her habits and began to try and housebreak her all over again. But Lulu got progressively worse, to the point of actually eating her own feces and licking her urine.

Their veterinarian diagnosed the problem (coprophagy) as a diet deficiency and prescribed supplements and charcoal tablets. After three months of treatment, Lulu was no better. She was extremely nervous and along with consuming her feces, she had begun to sleep in it as well. That's when they brought her to me.

Lulu was a pathetic sight; bedraggled, nervous and extremely thin. Although she was left for therapy training, I never worked on her habit of eating feces. Her diet, regular dog food without supplements.

I have found that the more mentally and emotionally disturbed a dog is, the more they are inclined to have unclean toilet habits. In milder cases, they tend to step in and walk through their eliminations without regard. Sleeping in the feces and eating them are indicative of

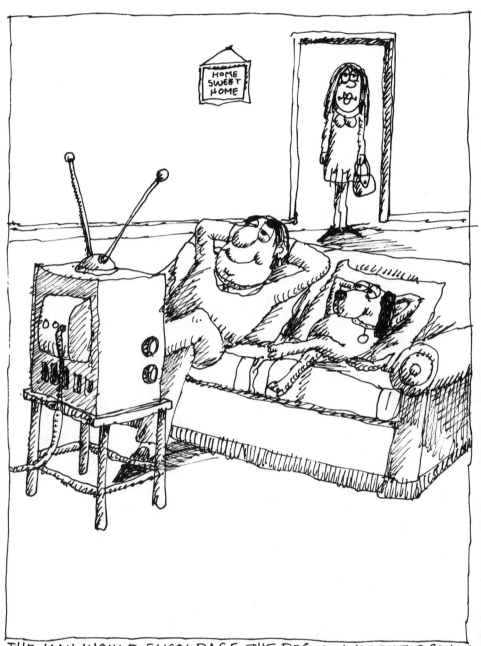

THE MAN WOULD ENCOURAGE THE DOG TO LAY ON THE COUCH...

more severe disturbances. However, when the mental and emotional aspects of a dog's behavior are balanced through training, they will automatically respond in the physical sense with cleaner habits.After six weeks of therapy training, Lulu had not only stopped ingesting her feces, she avoided any physical contact with it. By the time her training was completed, Lulu had regained her health, weight and tranquility.

I explained to the couple that Lulu was extra sensitive, and Joan consented to "bend" a little more and not be so harsh with her discipline. Dave agreed to stop undermining Joan's efforts. With the two of them working together, Lulu was able to function on an even keel. And for that, everyone was grateful.

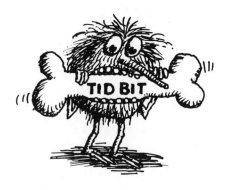

*Our emotions (or lack of them) can be
a very strong influence on our dogs' behavior.*

Rommel

"His name is Rommel," Mrs. Schuler introduced me to her German Shepherd. "I'd like to be able to show him eventually. I saw in your ad that you do that type of training."

"Yes, that's right."

"I believe he's an exceptional dog, but do you see how he carries his tail? I haven't been able to correct that. We'd never have a chance in the conformation ring if he looked like that."

Rommel was indeed a beautiful dog. At seven months of age he already showed real potential as a show dog. It was the way he carried his tail, held tight as a steel trap between his legs, that ruined his overall appearance.

"You're absolutely right," I said. "I don't think that should be too difficult to correct, however. He's young yet. The problem might even work itself out through basic obedience training."

"If he learns nothing else but to hold his tail properly, I would be happy," she said, and made arrangements to leave Rommel for training.

After Mrs. Schuler left, I hooked up a leash to Rommel's collar and walked him around the training ring. I talked soothingly to him and tried trotting a little to see if his tail would come out—it didn't. I put him in his run. Later that day, I happened to check on him through one of my observation peepholes to see how he was. Alone and relaxed, Rommel's tail hung down normally. It was a promising sign. I'd have that tail up and waving like "Old Glory" in no time, I thought.

Two weeks later, Rommel was progressing with the training. Learning the commands was the least of his troubles. However, he seemed always to be a little apprehensive of me, and his tail still clamped tight as ever between his legs. I hadn't been harsh with him in any way, and I felt he should have become accustomed to me by then.

One afternoon Roger, a friend of mine, and Luanne, his girl-friend, stopped by to visit me. Invariably, the subject of training came up, and I mentioned Rommel and his problem. Then I had an idea.

"Roger, could you and Luanne help me try something with Rommel?"

"Like what?" Roger asked.

"I'd like to have each of you walk past him while I watch out of sight to see what his reactions are to strangers."

They agreed to help me and we all headed for the kennel. I normally do not let people in where the dogs are kept, but this was an exception. I first directed Luanne to walk silently past Rommel while I watched through the peephole. As she went by him the first time, Rommel tucked his tail up slightly. As she passed him on her way back, his tail was down, and he watched her curiously. Next I had Roger do the same thing. As soon as Rommel spotted Roger, his tail instantly curled under, and remained tightly tucked up as Roger went past him a second time. It took the dog about five minutes after Roger had left to relax and let his tail hang normally. I went up to Rommel's run next and once again the tail went under. "Rommel, it's *me*," I said, and the tail drew up even tighter.

I pondered Rommel's reactions to my experiment. It was clear that he had more fear of men in general, than of women. And now that I thought about it, whenever I used his name to help him adjust to me, he'd tuck up his tail even more. I decided to try one more thing. I asked first Roger, then Luanne to say Rommel's name out loud. The dog's tail clamped underneath him each time with equal intensity. It was puzzling alright. I decided to call Mrs. Schuler and arrange a conference. Perhaps she could fill in the missing pieces.

"I've run into a little snag," I began as Mrs. Schuler settled into one of the office chairs. She looked at me.

"What's wrong?" she asked, concerned.

"Well, nothing is actually wrong with his ability to learn. He's progressing on schedule in that department. It's his tail tucking that is my main concern. I've found that he is somewhat fearful of men, and surprisingly, of his own name. I was hoping you could tell me a little more about his background."

Mrs. Schuler stiffened slightly. "Background?"

"Yes. For instance, how did Rommel relate to your husband in the beginning?"

"Not very well, I'm afraid," she sighed. "My husband is a wonderful, loving person—most of the time." She relaxed a little. "But several

ALONE AND RELAXED, ROMMEL'S TAIL HUNG
DOWN NORMALLY...

nights a week he comes home intoxicated. Frank is a completely different person when he's had too much to drink. He gets terribly loud and abusive. Before we acquired Rommel, I'd just retreat to the kitchen and ignore his ranting until he'd finally fall asleep in front of the television. But since Rommel came into the picture, he's the first thing Frank zeros in on when he comes home. He bellows out Rommel's name and if he doesn't come, Frank gets absolutely livid. Rommel really wanted to like my husband, but after Frank bounced him around so many times, Rommel would hide under our bed when he'd come home. That just infuriated Frank even more, so he'd get a broom and poke at the dog to try and get him out from under the bed. I feel sorry for Rommel, but I'm helpless to try and stop Frank when he's like that."

"That certainly explains his fear of men," I said.

"But why does he cower around me with his tail tucked under?" she said. "I've never given him cause to fear *me*."

"You say your husband calls out Rommel's name?"

"Oh yes. It's ROMMEL! this' and 'ROMMEL! that'. He curses that poor dog with every other word."

"Well, it's easy to see that your husband has created in Rommel a negative association to his own name. Therefore, no matter *who* says it, he's going to respond fearfully. That's why I wasn't making any headway in trying to gain his confidence when he first arrived. I kept using his name. No doubt you were trying to do the same thing."

"Yes, exactly. But what can we do about it now?"

"Normally, I would advise you to pick a new name for him. But would your husband agree to such a change?"

Mrs. Schuler shook her head. "Sober, he would. When he's had too much to drink, he'd go right back to Rommel."

"Well then, I'm going to have to change Rommel's attitude toward his name so that he'll respond differently."

"That would be wonderful!" She smiled sheepishly. "I should have told you about Frank from the start, right?"

"It would have helped," I said, smiling back at her. "But I can understand why you didn't. Besides, we've only lost two weeks. There's still enough time to get both his head *and* his tail straightened out.

Armed with this new information, I went to work on Rommel's new image. To start with, I gave him a temporary "kennel name." I chose "Muchacho," because it had a lively, sing-song pronunciation which was far different from the flat, authoritative sound of "Rommel." Every time I said, "Muchacho," I gave him a piece of liverwurst. He quickly learned to associate something pleasant with his new name.

Rommel-Muchacho made rapid progress with the training. It was not necessary for me to recondition his self-confidence directly. By removing him from his suppressive environment and using a different name, his confidence mushroomed on its own. It was heartening to be greeted each day with his furiously wagging tail, which he now carried gracefully wherever he went. Little by little, I began to introduce Rommel's old name to him while still using the liverwurst. By the time his training was completed, Rommel no longer reacted fearfully to his name. When Mrs. Schuler came for her training session, she was overjoyed at the positive changes in her dog. In our last session, she asked the big question.

"What's going to happen when I take him home and Frank starts in on him again?" she asked. Her voice was filled with concern. "I can't blame Rommel for being scared, but I'd hate to see all of this effort go to waste."

"That's a good question," I said. "He's much more stable now than he used to be. Let's just see what happens."

Around ten o'clock that night, my phone rang. I don't always answer that late at night, but I had a hunch I knew who it was.

"Mr. Meisterfeld? This is Mrs. Schuler. I just *had* to call you, late as it is, and tell you what happened. Frank came home intoxicated again tonight. I decided to stay right where I was, in the living room with Rommel, and not go off to the kitchen." Her voice grew excited. "Well! When he saw us, he started shouting and cursing Rommel as usual. I had told him that Rommel was coming home today, so I guess Frank thought he was going to put him in his place. He grabbed the broom out of the closet and came after Rommel. But you know what Rommel did? He raised his tail and fixed Frank with his eyes and let out a growl! Frank was so shocked, he just dropped the broom and stared at Rommel. Then without another word, he went into the bedroom and fell asleep on the bed, something he's never done before while inebriated. And after all that, Rommel just curled up, calm as anything, and went to sleep." Mrs. Schuler giggled. "Rommel looked rather pleased with himself actually. And why not? He won!"

Chindo

by *Major Jack Craft*

I first became aware of the Chindo breed shortly after my arrival in Korea in January of 1969. I read an article in a local newspaper which told the story of the dogs of Chindo (진 ㅗ 도) an island off the South-West coast of Korea. In ancient times, the Chindos were supposed to have saved Korea by barking at the Japanese fleet as it sailed by, giving the Korean defenders time to prepare themselves. More recently, the Korean people, wishing to protect the breed for as long as possible, made them the national dog of Korea and prohibited their exportation from the island.

The newspaper story told of their loyalty, cunning and intelligence, and contained a picture of the handsome fellows, who looked a lot like Huskies with their pointed ears and curled tails. There was a primeval look about them, especially in their faces and beautiful beige coats. The article praised their fighting spirit, hunting ability, and their reputation as ratters. I decided I wanted one of these dogs, even if they were very difficult to get off the island. I was at least going to try. I would have to wait, however, since I was posted to Vietnam for a six-month tour of duty, and would not be able to continue my project until my return that summer. I was assigned as a military advisor to the Korean Army and related my interest to one of my counterparts in Pusan, Korea. He was also interested in Chindos and agreed to assist me in trying to obtain a pair from the island.

My friend and I wanted to be sure our dogs were truly from the island—there were a lot of counterfeit "Chindos" around. If you let it be known that you wanted a Chindo dog, someone would come up with one—for a price. Then when they grew up you would find you had a plain ol' *Dong Kay,* or curr. (Direct translation is "Shit Dog.")

The arrangements were made, and my anxiously awaited "Chindo" arrived. When I first saw him I was very disappointed. What an ugly puppy! His ears hung down, his long tail drooped, his fur was short—he looked like a drowned rat. But he was different from any other puppy I had ever owned.

The puppy was about seven weeks old when he arrived and I was prepared to go through the agony involved in housebreaking. To my surprise, I found him to be *already* housebroken. When I told my friend about this miracle, he explained that Chindo mothers housebreak their pups themselves. By the time the pups are weaned, they are usually well trained.

I also began to notice that the puppy maintained a rigid set of standards for himself that I had not observed in other dogs. He would not eat stale food nor would he eat table scraps (except meat). Also he ate only at night and would not tolerate another animal near his food. He was, however, tolerant of human intrusion. He was also very selective about *where* he defecated. It was a special ritual to him. After finding the correct location, he would go into a circling pattern with his nose to the ground until just the right spot was selected. I have only seen this one other time; in a dog from Okinawa who resembled my dog so much that I felt they must have been related breeds.

I guess the most unusual thing I remember about him as a pup was that no other dogs could dominate him. When the bullys came around, they soon learned that *this* fellow was made of tougher stuff than other dogs. He didn't give in, he didn't beg, and he didn't run. Even at that tender age, when it came to fighting, it was not a game, but a deadly serious matter.

We named him, appropriately we thought, Chindo. He grew up spending his days with our *Mamma San,* and his evenings with Mary and me. He developed into a very beautiful dog, and grew to about fifty pounds. His ears peaked and stood up straight. His mane became shaggy, as did his tail which now curled around like a donut. He was the picture of a perfect Chindo. He never ate more than he needed, never got fat and now at eight years of age, is still the same. He loves to hunt (especially rats) but hates loud noises and car rides. He also has a very sensitive stomach—ever own a dog who throws up when he eats a bone?

From the very beginning he was independent to a fault, and also quite aggressive with his siblings in the neighborhood. He began to live up to the Chindo reputation by trying to fight every young dog in the area. I kept him on a leash always, and as long as he was controlled by that, or in the house, he was submissive. However, if he ever got off the leash, he didn't return until he had made the rounds of the neighborhood, challenging all dogs and animals. Then, when he was tired or hungry, he would come home.

There were several men in the neighborhood who owned hunting hounds (Korea is abundant with pheasant) and one fellow who lived down the street from us had a brace of them. He kept them penned up and each time Chindo came by, either on my leash, or on an occasional foray of his own, the hounds would raise holy hell. Chindo was about eight months old at this time and just about grown. The hounds were beautiful, full-grown dogs.

One evening one of the hounds had somehow gotten out of the pen and came upon Chindo and me while we were walking. The hound began barking, growling and became very agitated. Chindo was quiet and alert as he watched the other dog intently. I thought I had things pretty well under control because Chindo was on the leash and the other dog was not charging. The hound continued to bark and edge closer. Well, he got a little *too* close, and before I knew it, Chindo had the hound on his back with a firm hold on his throat. I had to choke Chindo down with the leash to make him release his hold; even at that, he had already laid the hound open before he grabbed his throat. I understand some dogs are slashers and some are chokers— Chindo was both, and he did it seriously and silently.

I don't mean to give the wrong impression about Chindo because he was, generally speaking, a warm and friendly dog. He never gave more than a warning growl or bark at a stranger. I think Bill put it best one day when he said: "Chindo acknowledges that man is superior and what belongs to man is man's; but he thinks the animal world belongs to him."

When he was about nine months old, I took Chindo to the United States. He flew over and I picked him up at the San Francisco International Airport. I was only able to keep him with me for about three months, then I was forced to put him in a kennel for almost a year. I visited him every weekend, and noticed that he was adjusting well to kennel life. The kennel was located in the beautiful countryside near Napa. The dog had a large run and a great view of the surrounding area. He even had a pigeon to catch from time to time when one would inadvertantly land on his kennel.

We were stationed in Oakland at the time and Mary and I finally were assigned quarters at Ft. Mason. We moved in with our two boys and brought Chindo from Napa. He has the ability to adjust rapidly to new situations and was soon settled in. It was at this time that he bit the only man ever in his life—me! I lost my temper with him and grabbed him by the flank and he snapped at me. He was always protective about his flanks and I should have known better. Mary and I immediately talked the situation over. We didn't want a biter, and we wanted a dog we could walk comfortably—one that would mind us and not try to attack or challenge other animals. Since we both worked we knew we could never train him ourselves, so we decided to find a trainer. We looked in the San Francisco telephone book and saw the Meisterfeld advertisement, called Bill and told him our problem. He told us to come right out to his ranch. Well, Chindo stayed with Bill for over three months, and when he came back home, we all understood one another much better.

After Chindo came home we had to adapt to the new situation as instructed by Bill, holding our emotions in check until we all adjusted. We really enjoyed our time at Ft. Mason, and from there we moved to Leavenworth, Kansas for three more wonderful years. We bought a house with a huge yard, had a fence put up, and gave Chindo the first freedom from the leash he had ever experienced. We had a great field behind the house with trees, birds, and rabbits. Coyotes also came down and howled at Chindo. There were plenty of dogs around for him to bark at, and we all had a grand time.

When the time came for us to go overseas again, we chose Korea once more, and are still there at the time of this writing. Chindo with us still, is older now, living in a seventeen-story high-rise. He is still trim, bright as ever, and again has adapted completely to his environment. He is quite famous here in the complex, in fact in this area. Our maid is proud to be seen with a Chindo dog. Our only real problem is people who don't keep their dogs on leashes. Chindo has been attacked several times and even now handles himself very well.

When we had only been here about three weeks I was taking Chindo on his evening stroll when we met a fellow with two dogs—a Collie and a mixed breed about Chindo's size. I pulled Chindo up and put him in a sit position. The other dogs lunged toward us and their leashes gave way. The only thing I could do was drop Chindo's leash, give him an "okay" and hope he survived. Those two dogs received the surprise of their lives. They couldn't seem to get themselves untangled from the fix they'd made for themselves. Chindo was everywhere. His massive head, neck and chest gave him a powerful advantage in protection and offense. My neighbor and I finally extracted one of his dogs from the melee, and we were able to choke Chindo off the other. I always hate to see this happen because the other dogs always get hurt when Chindo fights. The Collie needed

twenty-one stitches, the other dog had a lacerated neck. Chindo bit his tongue and had a lacerated ear. It took him several days to get over his stiffness—he's just getting too old for that sort of foolishness!

The Koreans are quite proud of him, and so are we. We continue to love him, and as he grows older he even shows a little emotion himself. Some day his facade may crack, and he'll jump up on my lap. I feel Chindo is a very superior animal, sensitive like a wolf or a fox. He trusts me explicitly. We have never hurt him, and he doesn't think anyone else will hurt him either. He has blind faith in man, yet he does not yield willingly if doing so encroaches on his independence. He is quite a dog; a wonderful, beautiful, living experience in our lives that we will always cherish. Bill, you are a big part of that experience because you helped us to better understand Chindo and "where he was coming from." Bill can tell the story about the training. . .

Training Chindo

It is somewhat difficult for me to describe what training Chindo was like, simply because he was so different from any other dog (pure or cross) that I have ever encountered. I believe he would have the ability to function in the wild just as well as he functioned in the domestic situation.

For Chindo, fighting was a way of life. It might have been easier to break him of it had be been motivated by his "ego," as is the case of most aggressive dogs who feel they have to be the leader of the pack. But Chindo was not a *macho* dog, with something to prove, and I'm sure he felt no malice toward his transgressors; he just attacked because that was the thing to do. It was as natural to him as wagging his tail.

Chindo demonstrated unusual—almost feline—behavior patterns. I remember growing concerned when he neither defecated nor urinated in his run for the first two days of his stay. Finally I put a leash on him and took him out in the field for a walk. No sooner did we set foot on dirt when the flood gates opened wide. After he had relieved himself, he scratched up some dirt, grass and leaves, and using his nose as a pusher, carefully covered up his excrement. It is possible that Chindo considered his run, with its cement floor, "home," and therefore off limits for eliminating. Or, perhaps he resisted relieving himself because there was no way for him to cover it up. He *did* learn to eliminate in his run, however, though I made it a point to walk him outside regularly. He was also an exceptionally clean dog, and it would disturb him if he accidentally stepped in anything offensive to him.

I quickly learned that his eating habits were nocturnal. We feed the dogs around five o'clock in the evening, then pick up their dishes in about half an hour. Some new dogs will refuse to eat at first as their way of objecting to their alien situation. I just pick up their dish along with the rest, and generally by the second or third day they will eat. Chindo would eat only a mouthful or two each day, and thinking he was probably protesting, I picked his dish up with the rest. I began to feel uneasy about him when after the fourth day he still would not eat much. I thought I would try leaving his food overnight. The next morning, his dish was empty. I realized then that I would have to be more flexible with Chindo, and that much of the psychology which applied to common dogs, might not necessarily be applied to Chindo.

In the beginning of Chindo's training program, I isolated him from the other dogs, and didn't work on his aggressiveness at all. He knew there were other dogs around, but he couldn't see them. I believe that the biggest thing in Chindo's favor was that he liked people, although he was not demonstrative or fawning with his affection.

We slowly developed a communication through the basic obedience commands, not using any type of reprimand for the first month. When I was certain he knew what I expected of him, I introduced the "nein" correction to let him know he was wrong when he would break a command. I also introduced some special commands to him. These were "be good," which was used when we approached a potentially difficult situation, and "leave it," which meant exactly that. I began by walking Chindo around the ducks and the goat. If he showed any interest in them as we approached, I would say, "be good." If he still persisted, I would then give him the "leave it" command along with a firm snap of the leash. I even had an unexpectedly good opportunity to use this command when we happened to encounter a large gopher snake. I really believe Chindo would have tackled *anything* he considered fair game.

When I could walk him around the ranch animals without him showing interest, we moved to the tough one—dogs. Chindo was not as easily persuaded to leave *them* alone, as he had been with the ducks. He had a genetic instinct to challenge any dog that encroached on "his" territory, and felt it was his duty to do so. It was extremely difficult for him to understand that it was wrong to attack other dogs, and this phase of his training was the hardest on him. His desire to please me conflicted with his natural impulse to fight. Fortunately, the former was stronger than the latter.

We used various dogs, starting with passive or friendly females tied to a post in the training ring, while I walked Chindo around them. As he progressed, I switched to passive or friendly males. On we went, until I could walk him within four feet of an aggressive, challenging Doberman male, without Chindo reacting. A more advanced version of this exercise was then used. I'd put Chindo on a down-stay (a very vulnerable position) and walk the other dogs around *him*.

It was a painstakingly slow process to get Chindo to that point. As Jack mentioned, three months of therapy training in all. But the biggest reward for me came *after* Chindo went home. Jack called me one day and proudly related an incident that had just taken place. He had had Chindo on a down-stay command in his back yard when his attention was diverted by a visiting neighbor. Some time had passed in conversation when all at once Jack remembered he'd left Chindo unsupervised. Jack hurried over to where he had left Chindo, in time to witness a German Shepherd Dog giving Chindo the sniff test. Chindo merely glanced at the dog and lay his head on his paws. Jack gave Chindo the "be good" command (to be on the safe side) before chasing the German Shepherd away. He then praised Chindo lavishly. Perhaps *that* was Chindo's greatest victory.

When Jack and Mary moved to Kansas, they wrote that they had adopted a female Beagle and named her Daisy. Soon she was accepted by Chindo as part of the family, and I am told they even played together. A Siamese cat named Thai was also a happy addition to their household. Jack found a good home for Daisy before transferring to Korea. But Thai, and of course Chindo, went with the family.

The story of Chindo's training would not be complete without mentioning the most important key—Jack and Mary themselves. Without their complete faith, cooperation, and love, Chindo's success would not have been possible.

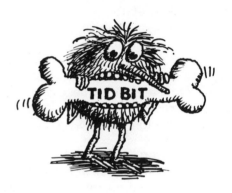

Dogs are the only creatures gifted
to serve us beyond the call of duty.

Two Plus Two

A long sleek limousine pulled into the parking lot and slowed to a stop. Even before the engine was turned off, the rear door flew open and two small figures darted out, disappearing from my line of vision. Hurriedly I exited my office and opened the kennel door. There was a uniformed man getting out of the driver's seat and a well dressed young woman emerging from the passenger's side.

I scanned the large lawn area for the other two, but could see nothing. Then I spotted a movement about halfway up the huge pine tree near the kennel. I ran over to it and found two young boys scrambling from limb to limb like monkeys.

"Get the hell down from there!" I bellowed. They both turned startled faces down at me, then at each other. As if by silent agreement, they reluctantly began their descent. The smallest one reached the bottom branch first, easing himself down until dangling by his hands, he dropped to the ground. He seemed uncertain of what to do next, so he stayed put until his brother reached him. Cautiously they approached me. They looked remarkably alike, although I would guess their ages to be nine and eleven. Their eyes were bright blue and wide with apprehension.

"What are your names?" I asked.

"I'm Mark," said the biggest. Then pointing a thumb at his brother, "He's Josh."

"Well Mark and Josh, there's something we'd better clear up right now. I don't want you two running all over the place and possibly getting yourselves hurt. You're here to learn how to handle your dogs, not to play games. Understand?" They nodded vigorously, their dark tousled heads bobbing. "Good. Now let's get to work."

This was to be the first of many sessions I was to have with the Sterling boys. Mr. Vincent Sterling, I learned, was a wealthy cattleman

from Novato (a small city nine miles south of Petaluma) who had large cattle herds in many western states. It was his secretary who made the arrangements for the training. He had two eight-month-old McNabs, which are short-haired herding dogs. She explained that the dogs belonged to Mr. Sterling's sons, who were going to work with them.

The two dogs had arrived driven by the same congenial chauffeur that later brought the boys and their governess. Ah, to lead a dog's life, I thought: to have the best of care, be chauffeur-driven, and even be sent to boarding school. I'm sure those dogs never realized their good fortune.

Their training went smoothly and was completed within the eight-week time period. They were good dogs, willing to learn and eager to please. I knew very little about the boys, but I hoped I would have as much luck with them as I'd had with their dogs.

Mark and Josh followed me in silence as we walked back to the kennel. I could see an exchange of astonished looks between the chauffeur and the woman as we approached.

"Mr. Meisterfeld," the chauffeur began. "this is Miss DuBois, the boys' governess."

"Ow do you do, Monsieur," she said with a lovely French accent. She had a round, pretty face, and her chestnut colored hair was secured in a small knot on the top of her head. "Just call me René."

"It's a pleasure. I hope you'll excuse me for running right past you, but I thought I'd better round these two up before they got into trouble."

"Zat ees quite alright," she chuckled. "Zey are full of mischief. I am always busy wis zem."

"Well, I guess we can get started," I said briskly. "Would you two like to watch?"

Miss DuBois smiled and glanced quickly at the chauffeur. "Oh no, Monsieur, I do not sink you need us. You seem to do so fine by yourself."

I told them that the session would take about two hours as I needed time to explain the fundamentals. With a final admonition to the boys to "listen and behave," they left.

Mark and Josh followed me into the training area where I motioned them toward the couch. I had a hunch these children were not accustomed to too much discipline. The time they had with their parents was probably limited, and Miss DuBois was hardly a match for these two dynamos. I began my spiel with a pleasant but firm tone.

"The first thing I should explain is that these sessions are important. How well you do is going to depend on how well you can follow my instructions. Your dogs are fully trained, they know the commands and what they're supposed to do. The purpose for these sessions is teach *you* how to work with them properly." Mark and Josh exchanged wary looks.

I went on to explain the various verbal commands, hand signals, what they meant and how the dogs would respond to each one. "Do you have any questions?" I asked when I'd finished. They shook their heads. "Okay, which one of you would like to start first?" Without hesitation they both pointed at each other. "Oh come on now!" I laughed. "It's not *that* bad. This is all new to you, but you'll get the hang of it before you know it. Now who would like to start first?"

"Let Josh go first," said Mark.

"No!" Josh shot back with a worried look. "You *always* make me do stuff first!"

"Hold it," I interrupted. "I'll tell you what. I'll bring out a dog and whoever it belongs to will be first. Since I don't know which dog belongs to whom, it'll be fair and square. Agreed?" They nodded solemnly.

I disappeared behind the wall where the runs were, and emerged with the dog I had picked. Mark let out a loud groan. No need to ask which one Pepper belonged to. I circled the ring a couple of times, demonstrating everything I had explained before.

"Okay Mark, come on over here and take the leash." I looked at Josh. "You watch closely so that when it's your turn you'll be perfect." I gave him a reassuring wink. Mark shuffeled over reluctantly and took the leash from me. Pepper jumped up, excitedly greeting his long lost master.

"Just ignore that for now, Mark. That's normal. Step off with a ' heel ' and keep going." When Mark followed my directions, Pepper quieted down and settled into the proper heel position.

"Halt." I said. He stopped and the dog sat. Mark gave me a look of astonishment. I'm sure he never expected to wield such power. The rest of the session went well. Josh too was amazed at the Svengali-like control he now had over Waldo. And I was pleasantly surprised at how quickly the boys had caught on.

When their time was up, Miss DuBois and the chauffeur had not yet returned for them. "Well it looks like we've got some extra time. How would you boys like to come down and see the pond?"

"Yeah!" they both chorused excitedly.

It was a beautiful warm day and the pond was like mirrored glass. We skipped rocks on the surface for awhile, then I showed them where we kept the ducks and Matthew, the goat. Presently their governess returned for them and they left.

Nice kids, I thought. Everything had turned out fine in spite of our dubious beginning. And the boys were obviously impressed with the control they had over their dogs. They were practically floating when they left.

When Mark and Josh arrived the next day for their second session, it wasn't hard to tell they were eager to get started. They giggled and fidgeted as I exchanged pleasantries with the chauffeur and their governess, who then left us to our work.

All went well for the second workout. Mark and Josh, in a very short time, were gaining much self confidence in working with their dogs. When Miss DuBois returned, we set a date for the last session— the day the boys would take their dogs home. We planned it on a rare day off for Mr. and Mrs. Sterling so they could attend the "graduation."

When the appointed day arrived and I spotted the familiar limousine coming up the lane, I noticed a quickening in my pulse rate. I was about to meet *the* Mr. Vincent Sterling, a real-life cattle baron. I had conjured up childhood memories of rich cattle barons, immaculately dressed, with silver and turquoise bands around their cowboy hats, hand tooled leather boots, and six inch cigars. They always said, "Howdy podner." I didn't know how much of this image Mr. Sterling fit, but I was nonetheless eager to meet him.

I approached the car as it pulled to a stop, and was greeted by Mark's cheerful, "Hi Mr. Meisterfeld."

"Me too," said Josh as they filed past me. I shot a quick glance in the rear of the car. There was no Mr. Sterling.

"I am sorry Monsieur," said Miss DuBois as she got out of the front seat. "Ze Sterling's had to make an unexpected trip to Arizona yesterday. Zey ask me to send you zere apologies for not coming. Zey wanted very much to be here, but. . ." She shrugged and smiled.

"That's all right," I said feeling slightly disappointed. "It wasn't a must for them to come, I just thought they might like to watch the last session."

"Oh, I almost forgot somezing," she said opening her purse. "Here ees a check for your services. Monsieur Sterling added payment for an extra training session."

"He did? But the boys are doing great. They don't need anymore training sessions. In fact I wish some of my *adult* clients were so cooperative."

"Well, he thought it would be wise for ze boys to have a follow-up, to see how zey are doing at home."

"Oh," I said slightly puzzled. "I guess a little reinforcement never hurts."

During the next two months, Mark, Josh and their dogs returned to the kennel twice a week for training sessions. I never did get to meet their father. The last few sessions found us doing advanced off-leash work with silent (hand) signals. Even *I* was amazed at how far they had progressed. The boys had turned out to be wonderful handlers. But even though I thought their performance exceptional, Miss DuBois would always request another session on behalf of her employer. She repeatedly assured me there were no problems with the dogs at home, just that Mr. Sterling thought it best to send them back for reinforcement. But I felt there was another reason, one that they weren't telling me about. I had to find out what it was, and when they came for the next session, I did.

"René," I began hesitantly. "these boys and their dogs are about as polished as they can be. If they ever went into competative obedience, they'd probably win hands down. So why all the extra sessions? There's really nothing more I can teach them, and I feel that to continue would not be professionally ethical."

"Oh but you are mistaken, Beel," she said seriously. "Zis whole experience had been most helpful to ze Sterlings and to me, not to mention ze dogs. You see, Mark and Josh have behaved so much better since zey have been coming here to work wis you. We were all so amazed at ze change in zem. Zey are good boys, but zey could be wild at times, as you saw ze first day. I must say I have had my hands full wis zem. But now. . ." she smiled. "What can I say? Zey are so grown-up! Zey are so serious about zere dogs. Mark, he tells his dog what to do now instead of little Josh. And Josh bosses his *own* dog, and for ze first time he feels important. Of course zey are still boys, but ze responsibility has done much good for zem. Perhaps we should have explained to you our reasons for coming so often, but we did not know if zat was wize."

"Well if that doesn't beat all!" I said incredulously. "I just couldn't figure out what was going wrong. Please thank Monsieur—I mean, Mr. Sterling for me, and tell him that this will be the last session. If the boys ever need a refresher course, which I doubt, call me. But for now, if I polish them anymore, they're liable to lose their skins." René smiled knowingly.

I said good-bye to Miss DuBois and the boys and watched the elegant limousine drive away for the last time.

Dynamite. . . !

I have my limitations, no doubt about it. My only problem is that I don't always know when I reach them. Maybe it was this blissful ignorance that prompted me to take on Dynamite, a year-old Black Labrador Retriever, for training.

"Well, she's a might shy of strangers, you know?" was the beginning of Mr. Albert's description of Dynamite. It was our first phone conversation.

"That should work itself out once she gets into her duck work," I answered confidently. "Probably just needs an ego boost."

"Ah, well, she don't take to gun-shots. Kinda makes her skittish you know?"

"Oh? She's gun-shy then."

"Yep. Don't seem to like birds either. Won't go near 'em in fact."

"I see." I began to get a sinking feeling. "Uh, have you tried her on a bumper retrieve?"

"Hah! She wouldn't fetch to save her hide. Oh yeah, she's scared stiff o' water too. Just trembles an' shakes all over, you know?

"Mr. Albert, are you sure you want *this* dog trained for duck hunting?"

"Yep. She's the only one I got and I kinda like 'er. Git along better with her than I do my wife," he chuckled. " 'Sides, I always wanted a duck dog."

There didn't seem any point in arguing his choice. "Well, bring her over and I'll take a look at her. I'll be able to check her responses for you and we'll see where we can go from there, okay?"

"Righto."

I sat at my usual office "lookout" post and waited for Mr. Albert's arrival. I wondered just how much the man was exaggerating. It just didn't seem possible for one dog to have so many problems. At least

I'd never seen one. Presently a slightly battered station wagon pulled into the parking lot. A tall hulk of a man emerged from the drivers side wearing a cream-colored cowboy hat. He ambled around to the back door, opened it and hunched inside. I had a clear view of the man's back; bent legs, shirt popping out the top of his jeans. He stayed that way for several seconds, jerking and twitching. It appeared he was having some difficulty. I decided to meet him outside.

Approaching the car, I could see he was in the process of prying a terrified dog off the back seat. Finally, grabbing the dog with huge hands, he picked her up and deposited her on the ground. The man straightened up and looked at me surprised. "Oh, Mr. Meisterfeld, how d'ya do? I'm Fred Albert." His face broke into a craggy smile as he offered his hand.

"Don't tell me," I said. "She's car-shy too."

"You guessed it." He grinned.

The dog, clearly shaken from the ride, spotted me and shimmied under the car. "DYNA!" Mr. Albert boomed. You come out from there!" He got down on all fours and managed to get hold of the leash and haul the dog out. "This here's Dynamite," he announced.

"Yes," I smiled. "I would have known her anywhere." Without preliminaries, I pulled out a small feather dummy from my back pocket and showed it to Dyna. The dog backed away suspiciously behind her owner's legs. I looked at Mr. Albert. "I see what you mean. Wonder what she's got against feathers."

Mr. Albert shrugged innocently.

"Let's see what *live* feathers will do for her," I said. I called for Larry, my assistant, to bring me a shackled pigeon (that is, a pigeon with its wings and legs bound), which I placed on the grass. I asked Mr. Albert to walk the dog past it. When Dyna neared the bird she bolted fearfully. Mr. Albert took a firm hold of her collar and tried to bring her up close to the bird, But Dyna writhed and twisted in panic.

"Wait, wait, Mr. Albert! You don't have to *make* her do it. That only reinforces her fears. I'm just testing her reactions for now." He backed off, slightly embarrassed. I was beginning to suspect that this was not the first time he had tried to force his dog to do something.

I had Larry release the pigeon, then walk out into the field about 100 feet away from us. "Okay, Larry, when I give the signal I want you to fire the training pistol once. Mr. Albert, I'd like you just to stand still so I can watch Dyna, okay?"

"Gotcha."

I gave the signal and Larry fired. There was a sharp crack. Dyna ducked low and spun away from the direction of the noise.

"LET'S SEE WHAT LIVE FEATHERS WILL DO FOR HER"...

"That's all, Larry," I called. Turning to Mr. Albert, "I have one more test I'd like to make on Dyna. Would you mind waiting here while I take her down to the pond?"

"No sir, you go right ahead."

I pulled my boots on and took the leash from Mr. Albert. Dyna followed, not willingly, and as far from me as the leash allowed. I could not—even remotely—imagine a more unlikely prospect for a duck dog. But fair's fair. Perhaps she would surprise me on this last test.

There are different degrees of depth built into the pond for different degrees of progress. I took Dyna to the puppy starting area where the water is shallow at first, then gradually deepens further out. I waded in slowly, testing to see how far she would go. But Dyna planted her front paws into the grass and strained on the end of her leash. Six feet was close enough for her. I walked her away from the water, circled and tried again, but she would have none of it.

As I headed back toward the kennel, and an anxious Mr. Albert, I tried to think of a way to tell him his dog was a hopeless mess. I had never seen so many fears in one animal.Maybe I could help, I thought, if she was just gun-shy, or water-shy, or . . . wait a minute! What if I took each fear, isolated it, and worked on each one separately? After all, I had delt with each problem before in other dogs. The only difference here was that they're all in *one* dog. Yes, it just *might* work. But first I had some questions for Mr. Albert. There seemed to be some pieces missing somewhere.

"Have you tried to work with Dyna at all, Mr. Albert?" I asked as we approached him. My question seemed to have caught him off guard.

"Well . . . yessir I have. For about the past six months, matter of fact."

"And what sort of training methods were you using?"

"The ones in the book. Just a second, I'll show you." He went to his car and came back holding something. "This book here," he said, handing it to me.

I leafed through, studying it briefly. "I think I see what the problem is then," I said, handing it back. "That book is fine for training *certain types* of dogs. I noticed several force training methods in there, and a balanced dog can absorb a certain amount of mishandling without any ill effects. But Dyna is *extra* sensitive, so any type of force or pressure in training will only create a negative response. In her case, it's fear."

I went on to explain that he had created a sort of chain reaction from the start when he had tried to force Dyna to retrieve a bird. From then on, anything new that Mr. Albert tried to introduce was—in her mind—cause for alarm. Thus it was not the birds, or the water, or even the car that Dyna feared, but the fact that her owner introduced it and she was afraid of making mistakes and being reprimanded. It took me quite a while to thoroughly explain all this to Mr. Albert.

"I think I can help Dyna," I said finally. "I can't guarantee you'll have a duck dog, but I'll give it my best shot."

"I'd appreciate it. I'd sure like to have me a duck dog."

Mr. Albert filled out a contract and we set up appointments for his training sessions. After making a small deposit, he left. I watched his car drive away, then opened my desk drawer and pulled out a piece of lined paper. I made a list of Dyna's fears and hung it on the wall in front of her run. It would serve as a reminder—and a challenge.

One of the first things I learned was that Dyna had developed a negative association to her name. I had no doubts that Mr. Albert had used it liberally while reprimanding her. I decided not to use her name at all in the beginning and instructed my assistant to do the same. Instead, to attract Dyna's attention, we used a bobwhite whistle. When she responded by coming in or out of her run, we tossed her a piece of liverwurst. For four days this was the extent of her human contact, except for feeding time, as I wanted her to have a period of unpressured adjustment to her new surroundings.

By the fifth day, I felt we were ready to begin the development of her self-image. For this purpose I employed the services of Little Orphan Annie, a small, rag-moppish dog that wandered to our kennel gates one foggy morning. Apparently, she had been abandoned, and was a pitiful sight. We took her in, gave her a bath and a hot meal. Inevitably, she adopted us, and we made her our mascot.

I discovered in Little Orphan Annie a talent that has earned her the position of "Kennel Therapist." She has a knack for getting along with all types of dogs, from shy to aggressive. They find her irresistible. Her gift has helped many a pampered, humanized dog begin to relate to their own kind. Now Dyna needed her help.

I placed Annie in the empty run next to Dyna, who had been set apart from the other dogs. Annie sniffed at Dyna through the fence and barked excitedly once or twice. She then ran inside her run and poked her head out to see if Dyna was watching. When she saw Dyna leaning against the run with her front paws, studying her, Annie barked once and disappeared inside.

Dyna's curiosity was aroused and—I'm sure in spite of herself— she let out a yip. That was Annie's cue. She came tearing out to the end of the run, barked twice, then ran back inside. Before she knew it, Dyna was caught up in Annie's enthusiasm and found herself joining in. Two days of this running tag game and Dyna began to loosen up and act like a puppy again. The next step was to put them together.

Never having been formally introduced, they were cautious during their initial meeting. But once they became familiar with each other, they were off on a day-long frolic. When feeding time arrived, Annie was returned to her run.

The next day I put them together again. But this time I went inside the run and gave five short blasts on my field-training whistle. Annie responded instantly by running to me. Dyna, who at this point would have followed her anywhere, was right behind. Each received a piece of liverwurst. It wasn't long before Dyna responded to the whistle command by herself. So far, so good.

Reintroducing Dyna to training was going to be a bit more tricky. I put chain collars on Annie and Dyna, then snapped each one to a separate six-foot leather leash. Together we ran playfully around the training ring. It was clear that Dyna was quite taken with her therapist. She hardly noticed me. The strategy behind this was to get her so engrossed with Annie that she would forget to be afraid.

We repeated this maneuver the next day but with the addition of liverwurst treats when we stopped. This was as far as Annie could take her. She had done a fine job, but now I needed to begin their separation while Dyna was still eager. In order for her to work for me, I would have to replace Annie as the object of her attention. I placed Annie two runs away from Dyna and by the end of the week, I moved her out of sight.

That afternoon as I approached Dyna's run, I gave the command whistle, and when she came I popped her the usual treat. While she was still savoring the tasty morsel, I hooked a leash to her collar and walked her to the training ring. Without Annie to distract her, Dyna—at first—showed some reluctance to come with me. But once I started encouraging her to run, she decided to go along. Five minutes later her first therapy session for the day was over. In the beginning I was not so much concerned with teaching her something as gaining her trust. It was going to be a delicate process. The slightest hint of pressure would ruin my chances of teaching her anything. During the early stages she had to be handled sensitively, and the sessions had to be fun for her.

For several days our workouts were just like the first, short and sweet. As she became more accustomed to me, I began to introduce verbal commands, *slowly,* using a soft but firm voice. The heel was first, then little by little we graduated to the others: stand, stay, sit, down, come.

Somewhere in these weeks of training, Dyna decided she sort of liked it, and looked forward to it. *Wagged her tail even!* I looked at the list I had made eight weeks earlier and scratched a bold line through "man-shy." I had just begun.

Working out her car-shyness was a little easier now that she had a certain degree of trust in me. I took her out to my station wagon at feeding time and put the food dish inside. When I gave her the "Okay" command, she would then jump inside and eat her meal. Several times after her training sessions I would put her in the car instead of her run. She really enjoyed lying on her special mat in the back, chewing on bones.

When she was completely relaxed just being in the car, I began turning on the engine for short periods of time. Later on I drove the car just up and down the driveway, and eventually, all the way into town and back, feeling grateful that she was not prone to motion sickness. I scratched "Car-shy" off my list also.

I have found that when a dog has been turned off by forced retrieving methods, it's best not to use anything related to the usual training equipment such as plastic bumpers (as used on the side of boats when docking), canvass dummies, birds (live or otherwise), sticks or balls. So I use meaty knuckle bones.

Now Dyna had developed a lust for juicy bones, as I often hand them out after feeding. Before we began our training session one day, I hid a bone on a window ledge in the training ring. I took Dyna out and circled the ring several times, stopping right by the bone. Dyna sat smartly. I praised her, unsnapped the leash and took the bone from the ledge. Dyna sniffed and licked it hungrily. Before she could grab it I threw the bone about 20 feet away and gave her a "take it" command. (She would have had a negative association to the "fetch" command, so I used "take it" for the time being.)

She ran after it and picked it up. "Good girl, Dyna! Come." I clapped my hands twice. She ran back to me and sat holding her prize. "That's a *good* girl! Now give." I took the bone away from her and popped her a piece of liverwurst.

As Dyna progressed, I gradually added to the bone. First I slipped it into an old sock. Then one duck feather was taped onto the sock. Gradually, more feathers were added until it was covered with them. Later I took the bone out and replaced it with a regular retrieving bumper with an 18-inch cord attached so I could throw it a greater distance. After mastering her indoor retrieves, she was ready for outdoor work. Dyna had learned to love retrieving, so I scratched *that* off my list.

My next step was to get Dyna over her gun-shyness. For this phase I needed some help.

"HEY! HEY! HEY!" Dyna looked curiously in Larry's direction to see what the yelling was about. He stood about 150 feet away from us. When he had her attention, he threw the bumper. This was the first stage before exposing her to the noise of a gun. After about six or seven retrieves this way, I motioned for Larry to use the cap pistol instead of the yell.

CRACK! Dyna paused, momentarily confused. Quickly I signaled Larry. "HEY! HEY! HEY!" he called out again. Dyna recovered and completed the retrieve. I realized that I would have to go a little slower for this one.

For the next ten days I varied the use of the gun, sometimes using only the yell, other times just the shot. When I saw no hesitation on Dyna's part, we dropped the yelling altogether and used a training pistol with a louder report. The range was also shortened each day until Larry was firing only forty feet from us, tossing the bumper to his side instead of directly to us. Dyna kept right on retrieving. A few more days and she was ready for the big one—the shotgun.

For this, Larry went back to the 150-foot mark, fired the training pistol and tossed a bumper. With a fetch command (which I had since reintroduced to her) she was off. She grabbed the bumper on a dead run and came flying back eagerly for another chance. I got Dyna ready for the next retrieve, then signaled for Larry to use the shotgun. He raised it to his shoulder pointing the barrel high into the air and away from us. BOOM! Dyna reeled in a circle and looked around, astonished. Larry threw the bumper immediately and I gave her the fetch command. She hesitated a moment, then shot off to pick up the bumper. I let out a sigh of relief. Only then did I realize I was holding my breath. It was another two weeks before I could do the shooting with Dyna alongside of me. When she was "steady to shot" using a 12-gauge shotgun, I scratched "gun-shy" off my list. Four down, two more to go.

Once Dyna got used to retrieving a full-feathered bumper, it didn't take much to get her to retrieve a shackled pigeon. I slowly introduced her to ducks by slipping small mallards in along with the pigeons. Then I quit the pigeons altogether. Next I slipped larger

I VARIED THE USE OF THE GUN.....

ducks in with the mallards and soon Dyna was retrieving the biggest ducks we had. Scratch "bird-shy."

The fact that Dyna had overcome most of her fears up to this point, had boosted her self-confidence considerably. In so doing she had made much progress in overcoming her fear of water. But not totally. Although she had enough trust in me (and faith in herself) to enter the water, she still would not swim. She made all shallow retrieves beautifully, but when the bottom left her, she would turn around and come back to shore.

I wanted to see if a lively duck might entice her to swim, so I took one that had its wings clipped and tossed it out just beyond the point where she stopped. Dyna waded chest deep, barked and bounced, but would go no further. At that point, I had to call it quits for the day. Larry picked the duck up in the boat, and I put Dyna back in her run. I had hit a snag in the training and needed to determine what the next step should be. We had reached a crucial point. As a duck dog, she would *have* to swim for most retrieves. Yet, how could I make her *want* to swim?

I remembered another Lab that I trained several years before. He had no problems of neurosis, yet he didn't have a very strong instinct or desire to swim. I had to trick him and it worked. Possibly it could work for Dyna too. I began to formulate a plan. . . For the next five days I left Dyna in her run with no work sessions. On the sixth day I took her down to the pond and tied her leash to a pole about 35 feet from the water's edge. Then I went back to the kennel and took out a Golden Retriever named Niki, whose duck training was almost completed. For the next 15 minutes I threw out bumpers for Niki. I praised him lavishly and fed him liverwurst after completing his retrieves. Dyna, who was nearly bursting with unspent energy, barked and danced for *her* chance.

I took Niki back, leaving Dyna still demanding my attention. Then I returned for her and put her up also. I repeated this for the next few days. When I thought she was just about prime, I got ready for phase two of my plan.

On D-Day (Dynamite Day) everything was set. As usual, I had Niki make a couple of retrieves. I then retied Dyna's leash to the pole with a light string so that when she tugged hard enough it would break.

I went back to the water's edge and signaled Larry to fire a shot from the pistol and throw a young squawking duck out into the water. Niki sat quietly waiting for me to give the command. I waited.

Dyna, in her frenzied excitement, gave a powerful tug and

snapped the string. Like a cannonball she tore down the slope and exploded into the water. She wanted that duck and that was all. The only thing she didn't know was that, at the point where I was standing, there was no gradual sloping into the water. It was the "advanced slope" where the bottom dropped away quickly. So before Dyna could stop running, she found herself swimming. Carried by her enthusiasm and energy, she continued toward the mallard.

While Dyna was busy swimming for the duck, I quickly tied Niki to the post and out of the way to avoid confusion. By then Dyna had made the pick-up and was heading back to shore. She sloshed out of the water holding the duck, trotted up to me and sat dripping. "Give," I said, holding my hand out. She released the duck and waited for my "okay" before shaking off.

Eagerly I signaled for Larry to shoot again and toss another duck. Without waiting for my command, Dyna took off for the second time. Her breaking was permitted and even encouraged, during the following retrieves. Within two days Dyna's fear and hesitancy of swimming was over. I then steadied her once again to retrieve on command only. Scratch "water-shy." Whew!

It had been twenty-two weeks since Dyna embarked on her reprogramming. At last she was ready to go home. I was eager to see the look on Mr. Albert's face when he saw how much his dog had changed. And he would have what he had always wanted—a duck dog.

When the appointed day arrived for Mr. Albert's first training session, I had everything in readiness. Larry waited, ducks ready, by the pond. Dyna was meticulously groomed for her debut. But the time came and went and Mr. Albert didn't show. I thought it odd not to have received a call or even a letter saying he couldn't make it. When he didn't show the next day for the second session either, I decided to call *him*.

I pulled out his contract and dialed the number he had written. Instead of the usual ringing, I heard a series of beeps, squawks, and clicks. Then a familiar recording, "Sorry, you have reached a disconnected number. . ." I hung up and tried again, only to hear that ominous recording repeat itself. I had a very uneasy feeling.

I dashed off a postcard reminding Mr. Albert of our appointments and popped it in the mail. A week passed with no response, so I sent a letter:

Dear Mr. Albert:

If you want me to hold Dyna for a while, I would appreciate partial payment. Please call me at your earliest convenience.

Sincerely yours,
C.W. Meisterfeld

Thinking he could possibly be on vacation, I waited another ten days. Still no response. By this time I was in a bit of a panic. How could this man go off and forget his dog? His *duck dog,* for God's sake!

My third letter went by registered mail. Shortly after I received the return receipt signed by Mr. Albert, showing a new city location in the Bay Area. Through information I obtained his phone number and tried to call. It was several days before I finally reached him late one evening.

"Mr. Albert?"

"Yup."

"Bill Meisterfeld. I'd like to talk to you about your dog."

"Lissen, mister," he said, suddenly angry. "I'm outta work, going through a divorce, I ain't got no money, and as far as I'm concerned I ain't got no dog either. You can do what you want with her, but don't bother me again." He hung up.

I stared numbly at the phone. All that work, the time, the frustration, the accomplishments—for nothing. I took the list down and added two more items: scratch one owner, and scratch $1000.

A few months later I found a reliable owner for Dynamite who more than appreciated her sensitivity and hunting abilities. I was glad. Dyna was a good dog and she deserved a good home.

Warning: Trouble Ahead

"Could you come to the phone?" my secretary asked poking her head around the doorway. "The party on the line says she is an old client of yours."

I had just about finished a workout with a Great Dane, so I took the dog with me and gave him a "down stay." "Hello, may I help you?"

"Yes, this is Mrs. Craig. You probably don't remember me but you trained two German Shepherds for my husband several years ago."

I remembered all right! I remembered that she had been extremely difficult to work with. She questioned just about every one of my procedures and refused to follow instructions. If it hadn't been for her cooperative husband, the training might have been a failure.

"The Shepherds are doing just fine," she went on. "They are a real joy to my husband. The reason I'm calling is that I've purchased another dog for myself. He's a five-month-old Golden Retriever. We're going away for a short vacation and I want to have you train G.B.—that's short for Golden Boy—while we're gone."

"That's wonderful. It's very possible he can qualify for the basic foundation training which is a four week course. . ."

"Four weeks!" gasped Mrs. Craig. "I don't want him trained for the show or anything fancy. We will only be gone for a week, can't you just give him a little training in that time?"

"A week isn't nearly enough time to train a dog," I said. "Even with four weeks of training your dog won't be completely finished. You'll have to spend at *least* another four to five weeks at home instilling what I've taught him here. I mentioned the four week course only because most young pups can handle it pretty well; unless of course they have a behavior problem."

I could feel undercurrents of hostility coming from her, even over the phone. At the same time an unmistakable "gut feeling" was telling me to back out, to discourage her from pursuing the matter. Training an uncooperative dog is difficult, but trying to work with an unco-operative dog *owner* is frustrating.

"Still . . . four weeks seems like a long time," she said. "He's awfully smart. Isn't there any possible way we could leave him for only one week?"

"Mrs. Craig, I would be more than happy to board your dog while you're on vacation, but I will not attempt to accommodate you with just one week of training. It would have absolutely no value. Why don't you give it some thought and call me back when you've decided what you'd like to do."

"Oh . . . well, thank you. Good-bye." she muttered.

I didn't expect to hear from her again, but thought it was just as well. Better not to get involved if there is no rapport with the person. I quickly forgot the incident.

A few days later, I was amazed to get another call from Mrs. Craig. She wanted to bring her dog out to me to look at and possibly train for the four week program. Although our conversation went a little smoother, I felt again the urge to back out. But as it happened, my intellectual reasoning overrode my intuition and we set up an appointment for a consultation.

Mrs. Craig arrived the following day. She hadn't changed much from what I remembered of her; fiftyish, thin, eternally smoking. I watched her approach the kennel in her brusquely purposeful manner. A subdued young girl, her daughter, followed dutifully behind. And there was G.B., slithering along on the end of his leash, casting furtive glances in all directions.

I quickly retreated further inside the kennel to the training ring and stood very still as Mrs. Craig stepped in. Without even moving my head I asked her to bring the dog to me. When they were about twenty-five feet away, G.B. saw me and bolted backwards in fear. I calmly walked over to him, took the leash from Mrs. Craig, and just stood still. G.B. was panic stricken. He pulled frantically on his leash in an attempt to escape.

"This is not normal behavior," I began. "His reactions are . . ."

"That's because of you," she interrupted. "You're a stranger to him. He's fine at home." She forced a smile.

"How long have you had him?" I asked.

"Since he was about six weeks old."

"Do you keep him in the house, or does he stay outside?"

"We've always kept him in the house. The other dogs stay in the back yard. But he's paper trained of course."

"THAT'S BECAUSE OF YOU", SHE INTERRUPTED.

"I see. Sometimes living a sheltered life with familiar surroundings can easily conceal a deep seated problem. Exposing a dog to strangers and unfamiliar sights will usually bring whatever the problem is to the surface."

Before she could reply, I gave the dog back to her and asked her to wait there for a moment. "I'm going to bring out another puppy about the same age as your dog. In fact I just started training her this week. I'd like you to watch her reactions compared to G.B.'s."

In a couple of minutes I returned with Abby, a five-month-old Collie, on leash. When Abby spotted Mrs. Craig and her daughter, she wagged her tail joyfully. Straining on her leash as we approached them, Abby sniffed at the two strangers, then turned her attention to greeting the other dog. Terrified, G.B. jerked the leash out of the woman's hand and sped away leaving a trail of urine as he ran. I felt that this demonstration would surely drive my point home. The two behavior patterns were completely opposite.

"G.B. is shy of other dogs," she stated flatly. "He's always been that way, even with our two Shepherds."

I started to comment but caught myself. I put Abby away instead, and by the time I returned to them, Mrs. Craig's daughter had caught G.B.

"All I can say," I sighed, "is that just by my brief observations, G.B. has some real hang-ups. To find out how deep they are, what kind of training he would require and for how long, I will need to work with him."

Mrs. Craig was hesitant, but finally agreed. As I watched her leave, I couldn't help wondering why she was going through all of this if it went so much against her grain. Perhaps she was at a loss about what to do with her dog and was angry at herself for having to ask for my help. I half expected her to change her mind and come back for her dog. But she surprised me when both her and her daughter got in the car and drove away.

Thoughts of Mrs. Craig diminished by degrees as I became engrossed in the task at hand. I worked with G.B. on and off; testing, observing, evaluating. His fear (of what appeared to be everything) was deeply ingrained. His behavior on leash was erratic, ranging from pulling me, to hugging the walls, to trying to break away, or just plain refusing to walk. When I put him in a run, he chose a spot in a far corner and stayed there. Normal behavior for a dog would be to sniff around, explore, try to see other dogs outside. G.B. displayed no such curiosity. Each time I reached to take him out, he would squat and urinate. I prepared an extensive list of my findings to discuss with Mrs. Craig when she returned.

"Boy, I'm sure getting tired of coming here," she clipped as she came into my office. I gave her a long searching look. I just couldn't figure her out. Oh well, I had walked into this one, and I was prepared to carry it through.

"I'm sure this will be your last trip." I said evenly. "Would you care to sit down?"

She dropped her cigarette on the cement floor and ground it with her foot. "No, no, I haven't the time."

I started to explain what I had found. "G.B.'s fearful responses could be due to lack of socializing with the outside world. He needs mental conditioning, not just emotional conditioning. It can almost be compared to kennelosis, a form of mental retardation that . . ."

"How much do I owe you?" she broke in icily, then began digging in her purse for her check book. Without another word I went to get her dog.

It was a shame she wouldn't listen to me, even though she'd asked for my advice. I wondered what would become of the dog. No use thinking about that. Even if I'd been able to help him, I would never have been able to work with Mrs. Craig.

When I returned with G.B., the dog again bolted fearfully when he saw her—just as he had when he first saw me. I coaxed him over to her and handed her the leash. He finally recognized her and they left.

As I watched them walk away, I realized that she didn't have anymore than before. But *I* gained some insight from the situation. The next time I get that "gut feeling," I'm going to *listen* to it!

... I WATCHED THEM WALK AWAY......

Figaro, Figaro

In the many years I have spent in the dog training business, I have been witness to some truly bizzare behavior, and I've also seen some pretty strange dogs. That's why I could remain relatively unaffected by the little drama that was taking place before me. It was the first training session for Figaro, a perky Beagle I had been working with, and the Passelli family, his owners. I had Mr. Passelli start off the session. I informed him, as I do all my clients, that the first session is the most difficult. The dogs are usually excited to be with family again, and the family is usually a bit nervous about making mistakes in handling.

Inevitably, Figaro had refused to respond to one of Mr. Passelli's commands. To my surprise, the man got down on his knees and, while cursing under his breath, began to hit Figaro with both fists. I quietly walked over to the scene. Mr. Passelli's face was red and twisted into a remarkable grimmace.

Figaro's face told me something also. If you can imagine a dog with a grin, then I would say that Figaro had the most self-satisfied "grin" I'd ever seen. In spite of his owner's repeated blows, Figaro appeared to be thoroughly enjoying the situation.

"Mr. Passelli? Mr. Passelli!" He slowly became aware of my presence next to him. "Uh, do you do this often Mr. Passelli?"

"Why . . . yes," he stammered. He seemed to have forgotten where he was. "It's the only way I can reach the bugger."

"Mr. Passelli, before you get up, take a good look at Figaro. Does he look beat?" The man studied the dog for a moment.

"Well . . . no. Not exactly."

"Or fearful?"

"No."

"The fact is he looks rather smug, wouldn't you say?"

"Because I punished him? Really!" Mr. Passelli gave an indignant laugh and stood up.

FIGERO IS MANIPULATING YOU.....

"No, not because you punished him. I would say that your dog enjoys the fact that he can get your goat. Figaro is manipulating you and that's what he's enjoying the most."

Quietly smoldering, Mr. Passelli listened to my deductions. It was a hard blow to his ego.

"Why don't you just relax for awhile, and we'll let one of your daughters work with Figaro." Mr. Passelli reluctantly turned the leash over to his twelve-year-old daughter and sat down to watch.

The thing I have found with children is that they are usually much easier to work with than adults. Both of Mr. Passelli's daughters took my instructions well. Figaro performed properly to their handling with no incidents. Mrs. Passelli sailed through her session as well. Figaro showed not a ripple of misbehavior.

By now Mr. Passelli was anxious to get back into the ring with Figaro. He witnessed the control the rest of the family had over the dog, and knew it was possible to control him without getting physically involved. Although he was eager, I wanted to make sure he'd have a good start.

"It's quite easy really," I said. "Let me show you the 'down' hand signal before you start." I took the leash from Mrs. Passelli and walked Figaro a few feet. We stopped in front of Mr. Passelli.

"Now watch. I take my left hand and drop it toward the floor directly in front of Figaro. At the same time, I give the 'down' command." I demonstrated the procedure and the dog sank to the ground.

"Okay," Mr. Passelli said impatiently. "Let me try it." He took off around the training ring and stopped when I gave the halt signal. Figaro sat. I felt inwardly relieved. Perhaps it was going to work after all.

"Down him." I said.

"Down!" Mr. Passelli boomed. He thrust his hand in front Figaro's face. He was doing it all wrong.

"No, the hand goes *down* while you . . ."

"Down! Down!" he repeated angrily as Figaro sat there looking dumb. The next thing I knew, Mr. Passelli was down on his knees beating Figaro, who had the biggest "grin" I'd ever seen. . . .

Plato advised:

"Let early education be a kind of amusement."

Rufus

"We brought him here as soon as we could, Mr. Meisterfeld. I do hope you can help us." The hefty woman plucked nervously at her dress collar. Her husband sat stoically next to her.

"I hope so too, Mrs. Azure. Why don't you tell me the whole story right from the beginning?"

"Oh my yes, from the beginning. Let's see . . . well, first of all I should say that our Rufus is a real smart dog."

"*Was* a real smart dog," Mr. Azure piped in. Ignoring him, Mrs. Azure went on.

"We always leave the front door open when the weather's warm, seeing as how we live in a small tract neighborhood and all. Well Rufus learned, all by himself mind you, how to open the screen door by jumping up and tripping the latch with his front paws. Then he just pushes the screen with his nose and goes on out. He can get back in all by himself too," she added with a glimmer of pride.

"Did you try to correct him when he began doing this?" I asked.

"Oh no," she said looking surprised. "We never minded him going outside, did we Millard? Rufus just likes to socialize that's all. We never worried about him."

"What do you mean, socialize?"

"Well, he just loves people and he runs all over the neighborhood, playing with the kids or anyone else he can find. He goes down to the shopping center about four blocks away and mills around there too. We thought it was such a friendly trait! And he's never caused us a bit of trouble in the last two years."

"One little thing you neglected to mention," Mr. Azure said dourly. "My wife tends to gloss over certain things." Mrs. Azure gave him a frosty look. "Rufus likes to chew," he went on. "Always has. If we ever have to leave him alone, he finds something to chew on. Oh nothing big, but enough to be annoying; you know, a shoe, a pillow or something." I nodded. "We just kinda figured it was because he was lonely and all. Well, yesterday morning we both had to leave unexpectedly. Rufus already took off so we left his eggs for him, and left the door open."

"Eggs?"

"Yeah, his breakfast. We don't know for sure if them eggs is what's doing it, but his coat sure shines since he's been eating 'em scrambled every morning." Mr. Azure's face darkened. "You better tell the rest, babe. I'm gettin' mad all over again." Mrs. Azure plucked even harder at her collar.

"What happened was that when we got back, we found that Rufus hadn't come home yet. His eggs were still there. Well this was just not like him at all. We waited 'till about one o'clock, then we went looking for him. Millard toured the shopping center while I drove around the neighborhood. Neither of us had any luck. We were quite worried about him, simply beside ourselves, weren't we Millard?

"Later that very same afternoon we got a phone call from a Mrs. Remer, who said she had our Rufus. She had gotten our phone number from his identification tag, you see. Oh my, how relieved I was! This Mrs. Remer then told me how to get to her house. I told her, 'Maybe if you just let him go he'll find his way home.' But she said she wanted me to come get him. As I think back now, her voice *did* sound strange. But I was so happy to know our Rufus was safe that I didn't really notice it then. I told Millard to warm up his scrambled eggs and I'd be right back." The woman paused and seemed to be summoning the strength to go on.

"Her house was about six blocks away and I found it all right. As I rang the doorbell I noticed that the screen door was identical to ours. The house even looked similar, being it was a tract and all. The woman came to the door with a face just as long as can be. She told me to follow her and she led me to a side window of her garage. I looked in and saw Rufus. I said, 'Yes, yes, that's Rufus!' and waited for her to open the garage door. But instead she asked me to follow her again. I thought she was acting awfully strange.

"She took me into her house, and down a hallway. She disappeared into a room on the left, and as I turned the corner myself, I absolutely froze. The room looked like a tornado had struck it! I mean to tell you, there were feathers, and gobs of what looked like hair, and broken pieces of pottery scattered everywhere." Mrs. Azure's face flushed at the memory. "She said that Rufus was responsible for the mess and that she was going to keep him until I paid for the damages. Why Mr. Meisterfeld, I nearly fainted! I said,

...RUFUS LIKES TO CHEW...

'Rufus did this?' I picked up some hair and looked at it. Mrs. Remer said that it was 125 year-old horsehair from the couch. I looked closer and there were holes chewed almost completely through it. Then I realized that everything in her house appeared to be antique. 'And how do you like the job he did on my antique Chinese table?' she says to me. The table was full of chew-marks and there were scratches and chunks of wood gouged out of it. On top was a shattered ginger jar. I could only guess that Rufus must have followed some kids and gotten lost. Then because Mrs. Remer's house looked so much like ours, he probably thought it *was* our house. But wouldn't you think he'd be able to recognize our scent, or rather the lack of it?"

"Since he is a Golden Retriever, I would think so," I answered.

"Phooey!" Mr. Azure said. "The only thing that dog's nose is good for is breathing. He couldn't smell smoke if he was on fire."

"Anyway, I don't know who started it first, but we both began to cry. We walked back outside and she told me to call her the next day—that's today—and she'd have an appraisal figure of the damages for me. She said when I paid up, I could have Rufus back. When I got home I told Millard what happened."

Mr. Azure took over the story then. "I called Mrs. Remer this morning, and she told me that our dog had done $2,200 worth of damage to her antiques. She said that Rufus was in a boarding kennel in a nearby town, 'So you can't get him back until you pay.' she says. Then she hung up.

"We only had $1,300 put away in our savings so that meant that we'd have to borrow nine hundred dollars to get Rufus back. I was tempted to let her keep 'im."

"Now Millard!" his wife scolded. "We borrowed the money and took it over to Mrs. Remer. After we paid her she told us where to find Rufus. So then we had to go and bail him out of the kennel too. This has been just awful, awful, awful! We brought him here as soon as we could."

"I'm glad you did," I said. "I'd like to work with him for a few hours if it's all right with you. Then maybe we can come up with a way to solve your problem."

"Oh, I *do* hope so," Mrs. Azure said. "We really don't want to give him up." With that, the couple left their dog with me for evaluation.

Rufus, as it turned out, was a beautiful dog with more than his fair share of charm. I found him to be basically sound but temperamental, and he also possessed a strong will-to-power. The only problem with him was that his energies had not been properly channeled; in other words, he was just plain spoiled. Three hours later, Mr. and Mrs. Azure were once again seated in my office, anxiously waiting to hear my "verdict." I gave them a detailed description of what I'd learned about Rufus' make-up.

"Now, in order to prevent another episode like this one, I have several things to recommend. First of all, you have to realize that your dog's misbehavior is something *you* have permitted. Even so, I don't believe that you're going to need my services as a trainer to solve your problem. I think all Rufus needs is some definite behavioral boundaries. This means you're going to have to make some changes.

"My first suggestion is to build him a run in your backyard where he can stay when you are gone. Also you should direct his energy into working sessions instead of just play. This will change the pecking order, making you "top dog," so-to-speak, instead of him. Make the training sessions short and fun for him. He's liable to balk if you work him too long or use too much force. He's temperamental and has been accustomed to having his own way. And *what ever* you do, *don't* let him run around the neighborhood anymore. Change the latch on the screen door if you have to."

"Oh that's just wonderful!" Mrs. Azure exclaimed. "We're so very grateful to you Mr. Meisterfeld, aren't we Millard? We'll follow your instructions to the letter, yes indeed."

As they prepared to leave I suddenly remembered something else. "Oh, there's one more thing." They both looked at me expectantly. "Rufus' diet should be just one kind—dog food. No more scrambled eggs, okay?"

"What ever you say, Mr. Meisterfeld." said Mr. Azure. And as he turned to leave, I could see that he was almost smiling.

Many of my clients have told me that they do not believe that dogs can reason, yet they continually place the dogs in circumstances which demand that ability, expecting them to determine what the right behavior should be and act accordingly.

Leroy

"His name's Little Lord Fauntleroy." Chuck announced, holding a wicker basket with a yellow ribbon tied on the handle. "Happy Birthday!"

Jo's expression was a mixture of curiosity and excitement as she carefully took the basket from her husband and peered inside. Peering right back at her were two large, limpid black eyes, surrounded by a flurry of silvery-grey curls. Jo gasped and reached in to pick it up. "Why, it's a. . ."

"A Teacup Poodle!" Chuck boomed, obviously quite pleased with himself. "Name's Leroy for short. Like 'im?"

"Well . . . I never in my life thought *you'd* ever buy a poodle, Chuck! Ooooh, how adorable!" she cooed, examining Leroy from all angles.

Leroy was somewhat dazzled with all the fuss and confusion. It seemed like only moments ago that the fearsome-looking man burst into the pet shop and pointed his big finger at poor Leroy, who felt like he wanted to hide. The dog's worst fear was realized when he was unceremoniously plucked out of his cozy little puppy pen, deposited in a basket and carted off by the man. But the woman's face that loomed in front of Leroy now, was a vast improvement, and he began to feel better.

Chuck gave himself a mental pat on the back. It was working out better than he'd planned. With Leroy to keep his wife occupied, he would be free to take his own dogs hunting every weekend. No more static about how he was always gone. Jo never fully understood his passion for the hunt; the wild exhilaration of bringing down the game; man and his beasts against the wilderness. It was a sensuous, primitive pleasure.

Chuck's frequent hunting trips had been a constant source of discontent since the kids had grown up and left home. Jo had always been so busy mothering that she hardly noticed Chuck's absences. But now, with increasing amounts of spare time on her hands, she'd been making more demands on him to stay home. Although he loved Jo and had nothing against "home" per se, he had—alas—been born with a restless spirit. Chuck tried, nonetheless, to comply with his wife's wishes, but his half-hearted attempts to do so had proven to be a frustrating experience for everyone. He was quite fond of his own dogs—Duke (a Weimaraner) and Taffy (a Chesapeake) and would let them into the house while he was home. Jo had put a stop to it, however, when Duke—ever the pheasant dog—pointed out her canary, and couldn't be persuaded to abandon his instinct. Taffy nearly wore a path in the rug, pacing from front door to back, making frequent detours to drink greedily from the bathroom toilet bowl. Chuck was just as restless. It was desperation that brought about the idea of a puppy for Jo, and only desperation would have made him choose a fluffy little Poodle to share his household with. He had always considered them "useless showpieces." "Gimme a *real* dog!" he'd say. "A *man's* dog!" So it was, with a touch of irony, that Little Lord Fauntleroy was going to be—so to speak—Chuck's salvation.

In the days and weeks that followed, Jo became increasingly absorbed in her new charge—and for good reason. Leroy had an engaging personality (at least Jo thought so), and he in turn loved his mistress dearly. He would trundle along after her as she did her household chores, and lay in her lap when she watched television. His compact size also provided an easy solution to taking him everywhere; Jo simply carried him in her shoulder bag.

When Chuck felt the time was right, he decided to broach the subject of a hunting trip he was planning. "Uh, Jo?"

"Yes, dear?" she said absently. She was matching newly washed socks while Leroy sprawled contently on her lap.

"I been thinkin'. Me and the dogs haven't seen too much action lately, so I thought we'd take a drive up to Tule Lake and do some duck hunting."

She and Leroy were now playing tug-o-war with one of Chuck's socks. "All right, honey," she said, giggling at Leroy's antics.

Next day Chuck was sailing along the highway in his camper. Taffy sat next to him, quivering with anticipation. Duke, sitting by the window, was just along for the ride. Pheasants were his specialty, and the season was over. But he was happy to be going along just the same. This was just the beginning, Chuck thought. There were deer,

DUKE, EVER THE PHEASANT DOG, POINTED OUT HER CANARY...

dove, quail, goose and pheasant seasons yet. And in-between there's always the clam and abalone seasons (Taffy and Duke were excellent clam diggers). And he'd be able to get them all. Yes sir, he was a real genius!

Meanwhile, on the home front, Leroy filled in all the empty spaces in Jo's day. He was an extremely intelligent dog, and he developed some rather refined preferences. For instance, he had figured out that riding in Jo's purse was by far easier than walking. And sleeping all snuggly and warm next to her was better than his cushion on the floor. And relieving himself in the house was infinitely more convenient than going outside. But Jo still thought he was the "darlingest thing," and didn't really mind his eccentricities.

The only drawback to this seemingly ideal setup was the tension Leroy created when Chuck *was* home. Chuck's opinion of poodles had not changed, and conversely, Leroy had not changed his opinion of Chuck. Chuck became increasingly annoyed when he'd reach for a pair of socks only to find gaping holes where Leroy had chewed them. It was also apparent that Leroy had a talent for getting himself stepped on. The first time was an accident.

Chuck had bent to kiss Jo on the cheek and happened to step on Leroy's paw. Leroy responded with an ear-splitting shriek that caused Jo to administer instant comfort, and Chuck to storm off in disgust. Since that time, Leroy made it a point to put himself between Chuck's foot and the floor whenever the opportunity arose. This of course was having a devastating effect on Chuck's nerves. Adding to Chuck's growing uneasiness was Jo. She hardly noticed him anymore. Sure he meant for Leroy to keep her company, but this was getting out of hand. His plan was working *too* well.

One night Jo turned down the bed covers and went to the bathroom to begin her nightly ritual of cleansing creams and moisturizers. Leroy took up his usual spot on the bed (Chuck's side) to wait for her. Chuck had resolved to put priorities—namely himself—back in their proper perspectives. When he found Leroy sprawled on the bed, he decided that this was a good place to start. Chuck gingerly picked up Leroy—who emitted his now famous scream—and plopped him on his cushion at the foot of the bed. Jo came running.

"You quit hurting him!" she yelled.

"I didn't hurt 'im!" Chuck hollered back. "I just picked 'im up and put 'im on the floor! And that, Jo, is where he stays from now on. I won't have 'im snoring in my ear another night! Understand?"

Jo opened her mouth to protest but the fierce look on her

NEXT DAY CHUCK WAS SAILING ALONG THE HIGHWAY...

husband's face made her stop. She stabbed him with an icy stare instead, then retreated, smoldering, to the bathroom. Chuck went back to the kitchen for a can of beer to celebrate his first victory.

Leroy, in the meantime, was all too aware of what had just taken place. He was not about to let this gorilla get away with such an injustice. He jumped up on Chuck's side of the bed, burrowed under the covers, and calculating . . . just . . . the right . . . spot . . . defecated. Mission accomplished he got down and scurried under the bed to wait for the fireworks. He didn't have to wait long.

Shortly, Chuck came in and undressed. Accustomed to sleeping in his altogethers, he turned out the light and jumped in bed. . .

"AAARRRGGHH!" It seemed he had barely touched in when the covers went flying and he vaulted out of bed. "LEEEERROY!" he screeched, and began searching for the little dog. Jo came running. She reached the bedroom and stopped cold. Her husband stood before her, breathing heavily, with clenched fists, clenched teeth, and a dangerous look in his eyes. Smeared along his backside and legs was the "surprise" Leroy had left for him.

"I'm gonna get the little S.O.B.!" he bellowed, and began to tear the bed apart.

"No! Please no!" Jo pleaded. "Please calm down. Let's take about it."

"Talk hell! This is *it*, Jo . . . this is the last straw!"

Jo's head reeled. She had never seen Chuck so angry. She just had to think of something fast. "Call Bill!" she cried, desperately. "I'll do whatever he says, only just *call* him. If he says to get rid of Leroy, I will. Okay, Chuck? Please?"

Chuck looked at her, teetering between anger and reason. "Awright!" he said finally. And so, at 11:30 p.m., without bothering to take a shower, Chuck called Bill and spewed out the story.

Leroy peeked out from under the bed and saw Chuck, the epitome of rugged masculinity, telling someone how he'd been done in royally by a Teacup Poodle, and felt a ripple of pleasure. He couldn't have known, however, that plans were in the making to tuck him away for a while in a kennel where Duke and Taffy had been before him.

Later that night as Chuck lay in bed, cleaned up and calmer, he began to reflect on the implications of what Leroy's absence would mean. He sadly made a mental note to clean and oil all his guns thoroughly; it looked like he wouldn't be using them for quite a while.

The Submariner

"Can you teach my Weimaraner how to swim?" the caller asked. I had gotten used to this question after working with numerous duck dogs who were afraid of the water and couldn't swim.

"Yes, it is possible to teach a dog to overcome his fear of water," I said.

"Oh Fritz isn't *afraid* of the water; he loves it! In fact I have a hard time keeping him out of it."

This was certainly a switch. A dog that loved water, but couldn't swim? The man brought the dog out and we went down to the pond to observe this wonder.

Mr. Moller tied a nylon cord to Fritz's collar and asked me to toss a bumper out for him to retrieve. I did. Fritz ran into the shallow water without wavering. As the dog continued toward the bumper, the water gradually became deeper. When Fritz was chest deep, instead of swimming which would be the normal tendency at that point, he simply raised up and walked on his hind feet. The deeper he went, the more erect he became, until just his head and paws were above water. Then Fritz disappeared from sight. Mr. Moller quickly gathered in the line and pulled his dog back into the shallow water.

"Does he do this *every* time?" I asked incredulously.

"Yep." was the man's simple reply.

"But you would think after almost drowning he'd be afraid to try it again."

Mr. Moller handed me another bumper. "Try it again and see for yourself," he said.

I threw the bumper and, sure enough, Fritz was more than happy to do his disappearing act again. He had no fear of drowning and made no attempt to save himself. It was incredible.

After Fritz was hauled to safety once again, Mr. Moller explained that the ponds at the duck club where he hunted were about three feet

HE SIMPLY RAISED UP AND WALKED ON HIS HIND FEET...

deep, and this was why Fritz had never learned to swim. The water was shallow enough for him to walk on his hind feet if he needed to. Mr. Moller learned of his dog's inability one day when he went hunting at a different duck club. The water was much deeper there and when Fritz went out for a retrieve, he went under and didn't come up. Mr. Moller had to jump in and rescue him. I assured Mr. Moller that I would do my best to teach his dog how to swim.

I fashioned a special harness for the dog and attached a long line to it. I tied the other end of the line to the outboard boat. When Fritz waded into the water and began to rise up on his hind legs, I would start the motor and slowly pull him until his body became level with the water surface and all four feet were off the bottom. In this way I was attempting to get Fritz to "run" on top of the water. When I saw his legs moving, I slowed down. If he started to sink, I would then increase my speed to bring him up again.

Fritz caught on quickly and began using his paws to keep himself above water. Within a few days, he was swimming on his own. No longer would Mr. Moller be afraid that his dog would drown, and Fritz could swim, and swim well.

Not all dog behavior problems are rooted deeply
within the psyche of the dog or owner. A case in point: Max,
a good-natured, easy-going poodle who was brought to me
because of a sudden personality change. He was becoming
progressively short-tempered and irritable, baffling his owner.
When the little dog came jingling through the doorway,
his two metal dog tags clinking together, I suspected
the cause of his disgruntlement, and suggested the tags
be taped together or riveted to his collar. The tags were silenced
and the problem disappeared—Max returned to his
"old sweet self" once again.

Palms Up

Everyone has his own way of evaluating a person before doing business with him. Probably the most common way people study each other is by watching the eyes, their social expressions, and/or by the strength of their handshake. But Mrs. Choy was different. She had made an appointment to see me about training her dog. But I was in no way prepared for our first encounter.

"Let me see your hands," she said as she stepped into my office. She was a petite, black-haired beauty, with a softly commanding presence. Her abruptness threw me off balance, and I automatically held out my hands. She turned my palms up and carefully studied one, then the other. I watched her with feelings of embarrassment and curiosity. What *was* she doing?

She looked up at me, beaming. "Yes, we do business." With that, she took a seat opposite my desk and sat down. She looked at me expectantly, as if waiting for me to make the next move. Now, I usually study a potential client to see how receptive they are to what I say. But this bubbly little Chinese woman had reversed roles so skillfully that, momentarily, I didn't know what to do next. I sat down.

"Tell me, Mrs. Choy," I said, attempting an air of nonchalance. "Why did you want to see my hands?"

She raised her eyebrows as if surprised. "I read your palm. First one show you lived a not-too-good life. But other hand say you now are good and can be trusted. You live honest life now." She smiled. She radiated an aura of unquestionable sincerity about her, but I must have looked doubtful. She went on.

"Bad hand show you were mean to people, even though you were kind to animals. You were selfish, always thinking about you first. And you could not be trusted. You were a sneak. Second hand tell me all that has changed now."

I didn't know what to say. I only knew she was scaring the hell out

...WHAT WAS SHE DOING?...

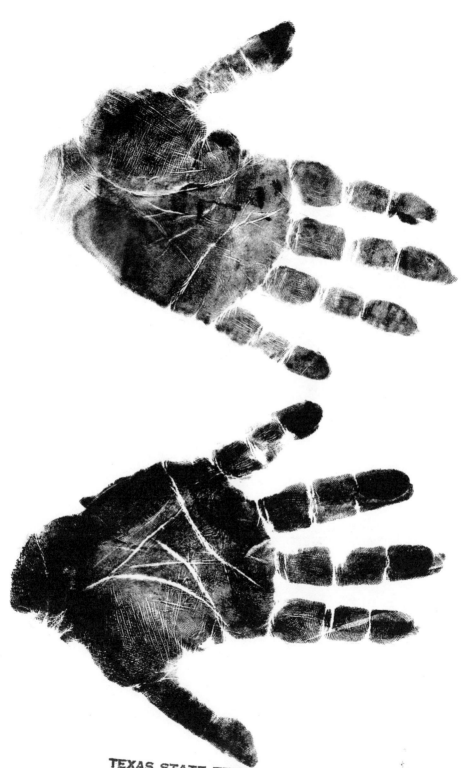

TEXAS STATE TECHNICAL INSTITUTE
ROLLING PLAINS CAMPUS – LIBRARY
SWEETWATER, TEXAS 79556

of me. She was right. As a youth, I had carried a great deal of resentment and hostility inside me. I had suffered tremendous emotional blows and by the time I was seventeen I already had bleeding ulcers. I had known the depths of despair more than once. Yes, it was a "not-too-good-life," and I had vented my anger in many ways. But finally, a turning point had come. I decided that I no longer wanted to live that way, and I took responsibility for my life for the first time. I began to change. It was an eerie feeling to think that my life's history could be etched in the lines of my hands.

"What do you do for a living, Mrs. Choy?" She reached in her purse and handed me a card. I half expected it to read, 'TRAVELING SEERESS, KNOWS ALL, TELLS ALL.' But it read, 'Oriental Imports and Exports.' I didn't dare ask her just what she imported and exported.

"Why don't you bring your puppy in so I can have a look at him?" I began to feel normal again as I walked her dog around the ring and gave him some simple tests. Yes, I felt a lot better.

"You work with my dog nicely. You know your stuff." She gave me a friendly wink. "I'll leave my dog with you I think, okay?"

As soon as I saw her drive away I went back into the office and studied my hands. How in the world did she know?

Romeo

Mrs. Ferguson's car moved down the lane, turned left, and disappeared from view. I sat quietly contemplating the scene long after she had gone. The parking lot gates were chained and locked as usual but one side was lying lopsided, unhooked from its hinges. The sign, "Open by Appointment Only," still attached to the gate, was now facing the ground. I suppose after so many years in this business, one should learn to expect the unusual. But I was totally unprepared for what had just taken place. I had vaguely suspected something was wrong when Mrs. Ferguson called that morning.

"How is my dog Romeo doing? I realize he has only been there a couple weeks, but I just *had* to call and see how he's getting along."

I could detect anxiety in her voice as she spoke. This is not unusual. More often than not it's the owners that suffer the most when separated from their dogs. "He's doing fine, Mrs. Ferguson." I said reassuringly. "He's eating well and has adjusted beautifully. He's turning out to be a good working dog and he's learning fast."

"Oh? Well I'm glad he's eating and all. I was just wondering. . ." she paused. Her words were slow and deliberate. "I wondered if I could make an appointment with you to see him."

"I believe we have already done that. Let me check my schedule just a minute and see."

"Oh yes," she said quickly. "We made one for three weeks from today for my visit. But I was hoping I could maybe see him . . . today?"

I felt my patience slipping. I can understand the concern most clients have in the first few weeks their dogs are gone, but sometimes their concern gets out of proportion. When it threatens to disrupt my training, I have to do something about it.

"Mrs. Ferguson, your German Shepherd bit two men because of his protectiveness over you. How can we possibly divorce those feelings if you visit him before he's ready? It takes time to modify an aggressive dog's behavior, and if you see him now he will revert, just like that. He *is* progressing on schedule, however, and he should be able to handle a visit from you on the date we originally planned." There was a strained silence on the other end of the line.

"I'm just used to having him around, is all," she said finally. More silence. "What is that date for my visit then?"

"The twenty-fifth at one o'clock."

"Okay, see you then. Sorry I bothered you."

Strange, I thought. I had explained all that when she and her husband came for the consultation. She seemed agreeable at the time. Or was her acceptance due to her husband's presence? That was possible. It seemed Mr. Ferguson was able to handle the dog without any problem. But he was very much concerned about the dog's aggression when his wife had him. Perhaps she did not share her husbands concern and was just going along with him. I finally dismissed the matter from my mind. It was only speculation on my part anyway. Even if it were partly true, Mr. and Mrs. Ferguson would probably have it worked out by the time her visit rolled around.

I had one more cup of coffee then headed for the kennel to start training. Beginning with the first dog in the line-up, I worked each one, making my way down the row and becoming totally absorbed in my work. Every dog is so different with individual needs, that I have to adjust my handling to each one. Very often my sense awareness and reflexes become so "tuned" at this time, that I sometimes know what a dog will do before he does it. This of course is a welcome bonus in my work. Perhaps it was this intuition which also make me aware that there was someone outside.

I gave the dog I was working a *down-stay,* and went to my office window to take a look. There was a car parked by the gate. Really nothing to be concerned about though—as long as the gates were locked. Many people drive by to try and see the kennel, but turn away when they see my "Open by Appointment Only" sign. All I need is for someone to pop in right at some crucial point in training a neurotic dog, and my work would suffer serious setbacks. Hence the reason for the sign. I also prefer a quiet kennel. A controlled atmosphere is essential for effective training, and unexpected visitors would disrupt the dogs. Generally after reading the sign and looking over the front of the building, people will drive away. So I went back to training.

I finished up my session with that particular dog and put her in the run. As I was putting the safety lock through the latch, I felt again that impulse to look outside. It was a good thing I did. The car was still there, but now there was someone climbing over the four and half-foot-high gate. The construction of the gate made it almost as easy to climb as a ladder. As one bare leg swung over the top, I realized that it was a woman. But I couldn't place her from a distance. Once over the gate, she put her head down and began a determined march toward the kennel. I decided I'd better meet her in the parking lot and find out what she wanted.

"May I help you?" I asked as I approached her. Without answering, she marched right past, as if I weren't there. Only then did I notice the leash and collar she was carrying in her hand. I hurried to get between her and the kennel door. She stopped when she reached me.

"What is it you want?" I said edgily.

She raised her head and glowered at me. "My dog." I thought for a moment she must have the wrong kennel. I didn't recognize her at all.

"Which dog? I have quite a few here." I tried to match this woman's face to those of my clients but I couldn't.

"Romeo. *That's* my dog, and I came to get him." It clicked. The voice on the phone! But it was hard to believe this was the same woman who had brought Romeo in. Her face, devoid of make-up, was drawn and white as if she had been ill. Her eyes were vacant.

"I'm going to take him home with me for a few days."

"Mrs. Ferguson, I tried to explain to you that that won't work. I'll have to start his training all over again." She spoke with a tremble in her voice. "I *said* I'm going to take him home with me."

I could not imagine what might have caused such a drastic change in her. Maybe, just maybe, seeing how well her dog was doing would bring her around. "Come in. I'll get him and show you what he's learned so far." I ushered her into the office to watch. I closed the door and turned on the radio to prevent the dog from seeing or hearing her while I was handling him. I took Romeo out and demonstrated the things he had learned in just a very short time. He did wonderfully. When I had finished, I took him into the office where the two of them greeted each other with tears, whines and kisses. Silently, Mrs. Ferguson took the collar off Romeo and put hers on him, then left the kennel.

I felt strangely removed from the whole affair as I watched her walk down to the gates. When she reached the gates she paused. Clearly, she was trying to figure out how to get her dog over. The slats

THE TWO OF THEM GREETED EACH OTHER...

were too narrow for him to squeeze through, and he was too heavy for her to lift.

At this point, I resisted the urge to go out and unlock the gates for her. Something told me not to. She didn't ask for, nor did she want my help. She had created the situation she was in and there was always a chance (however remote) that she would realize what their emotional relationship was doing to her dog. I watched expecting her to turn around and come back, at least to ask that I open the gates for her.

It seemed more than a coincidence that a rancher was visiting my next door neighbor just then. He had left the house and was just about to climb into his cattle truck when Mrs. Ferguson called to him. I couldn't hear their conversation, but I knew what was happening.

The man looked at the lock and then studied how the gates were attached to the post. He took hold of the slats, and with much effort, lifted the gate right off its hinges. Mrs. Ferguson and Romeo walked over the gate, got in the car and drove away without a backward glance.

Some behavior problems in male dogs, such as jealousy-related aggression, are approached from the wrong end (neutering)—the operation should be psychological!

All Flights Canceled

"Bill? This is Don."

"Well, hello, Don! How are you?"

"I'm not sure, Bill," he said hesitantly. "That's why I'm calling you. It's about Heather; I think I might have blown her training. I mean, I'm not sure whether I'm doing the right thing or not."

"Wait a minute!" I said. "Innocent until proven guilty, remember? What kind of Sausalito lawyer are you anyway?"

Don chuckled. "Well, I know all the work you've done to get her straightened out. She's been doing just great since I brought her home. Remember my telling you how she'd refuse to stop barking whenever the phone rang? Well, now she only barks once or twice to let me know it's ringing; but then she stops when I answer it. And she doesn't drag my shoes and newspapers all over the house anymore either."

"What about getting up on the furniture?" I asked. I could almost see Don wince.

"That's what I'm calling about. She knows I don't want her all over everything and she's been exceptionally good about that. But every evening she sits at my feet and pleads with those big brown eyes to get up on the couch. I felt sorry for her so I went out and bought her a loveseat. She's laying on it right now. But I began to wonder if maybe I had done the wrong thing."

I laughed. "You can quit worrying, Don; you're pardoned. I think that's an ingenious solution. However, you should make it clear that that's *her* spot alone. By the same token no one else should be permitted to sit on her chair either."

"Right! Man, am I glad to get *that* off my chest. I'm really pleased with her, Bill. Thank you."

Don had not mentioned the one thing I was *most* curious about, and I think I knew the reason he was holding back. "Don is Heather

AND PLEAD WITH THOSE BIG BROWN EYES TO
GET UP ON THE COUCH...

twisting her head again?"

He let out a sigh. "Afraid so, Bill. It seems that I had no sooner gotten her home when she started it up again. I still haven't found out what's making her do it, so I've just accepted it for now." His tone changed abruptly. "Hey, how about coming over for dinner next week? I'll show you the set-up I have for her and you can see for yourself how well she's adjusted. Okay?"

"Sounds great. I'd like that very much." After making arrangements for the dinner we said good-bye.

It was good to know that Heather was doing so well, but I was still baffled over the only problem we hadn't been able to solve. Heather had developed the curious habit of twisting her head back and forth continually as though she were watching a ping-pong match. This was the main reason Don had contacted me originally. I recalled our first meeting when Don brought her in for consultation.

"Why don't you start from the beginning," I told him. "Then maybe we can pinpoint the cause of her problem." Don proceeded to do so with an attorney's thoroughness.

"I'd been thinking about getting myself a good dog for some time. I'm a bachelor and I like to go backpacking frequently, so I thought a dog would be nice to take along on my trips. I didn't know what kind of dog to get. A friend suggested I go to the dog show at the Cow Palace, so I could see all the different breeds first hand, and also talk to the breeders. This I did, and I had not realized there were so many different varieties of dogs—all shapes, sizes and colors. There was also this one . . . this beautiful Irish Setter that caught my eye. I just *knew* that that was the dog for me! However, that particular dog was not for sale. The breeder, I learned, was from New Jersey, so I made arrangements for him to call me when his bitch had another litter of pups. Six months later he called to tell me that he had some pups for sale, so I flew out to the East Coast to pick one.

"I selected Heather, or maybe I should say she selected me, because she was the first one that came over to me when I went in to look at them. She acted like she had been waiting for me all that time."

According to Don, the plane trip back didn't have any ill effects on Heather, and in only three days she was housebroken. Heather had turned out to be the pick of the litter and Don doted on her like a proud papa. He built her an elaborate backyard run with an insulated dog house that had electric floor heat. She had nothing but the best.

"It was hardly noticeable at first," Don said. "But gradually I could see her twisting her head left to right, and back again. I took her to my veterinarian because I thought she might have ear mites or an infection. But he said he couldn't find anything physically wrong with her. He thought it might be just nervous energy and suggested I let her run more. I have a friend who owns a large ranch so I took her there. Well, she ran all right, but she also never stopped twisting her head."

At this point, an idea came to me. "Do you live near a tennis court or anything? A ball field where she could watch the balls being tossed back and forth?"

"No, I wish that was the case. My house is right on the water's edge. Besides, I had my contractor build rock walls alongside her run about fifty feet apart. I wanted to be sure that she wouldn't bark at everything that went by."

The consultation ended without my discovering what was causing Heather's head twisting. Even so, Don decided to leave her for obedience training as she had other negative behavior patterns typical of most pampered dogs.

The training went smoothly in that I was able to work out the undesirable aspects of her behavior. I proceeded under the hope that once I'd trained her, the head-twisting would disappear of its own accord. The problem gradually diminished and finally vanished altogether while she was with me. Because I had not discovered the *cause*, however, I was not totally confident that it had been erased for good.

The next week I arrived at Don's handsome "bachelor pad" for dinner. Neither one of us would have guessed that the mystery of Heather's swiveling head would be solved that night.

"Welcome, welcome!" Don greeted. "Come on, I'll show you around the place before it gets dark." The yard in front of his home was exquisitely landscaped with trees, shrubs and rocks. He led me over a natural stone foot path to the back of the house.

"This is where Heather stays at night and while I'm at work," Don said, pointing to a spacious run situated in the elegantly landscaped backyard. It nestled between two five-foot-high rock walls. Thick patches of berry bushes grew along the top of the walls. The floor of the run was done in flagstone, and the comfortable dog house sat at the very end of the run. The entire run was enclosed with chain-link fencing.

I whistled. "This is *really* beautiful!" Just then a quail flew out of the berry bushes on our right, landed on the opposite wall and disappeared. We heard his high-pitched call, and another quail flew across. In the next few minutes the quail were fluttering noisily to and fro.

SHE WAS STANDING AT THE END OF HER RUN <u>ALSO</u>,
WATCHING THE FLYING QUAIL.....

We stood there, delightfully watching them fly back and forth. *Back and forth?* I quickly looked in Heather's direction. She was standing at the end of her run, *also* watching the flying quail—twisting her head back and forth. . .

Don must have seen her too, for we both looked at each other at the same time. "It's the quail!" he cried excitedly.

"It sure is! I believe we've found the answer."

"Why didn't I figure that out before?" he said, perplexed. "The answer was right under my nose all the time."

Don explained that the quail visited his berry bushes almost every morning and evening, and that he enjoyed having them around. But he never connected them with Heather's problem. I didn't have to advise him what to do. That same week he had all the berry bushes removed. The quail didn't come around anymore, and Heather no longer twists her head back and forth, back and forth. . .

Ralph

I took Monty, the Bullmastiff, out of his run and, on leash, led him down the row of kenneled dogs. As we neared the last run, a small white dog bounded against the gate, barking at Monty. The big dog regarded him tolerantly. I smiled. Monty could have swallowed the little ten-pound terrier mix in one gulp—had he the inclination to do so. But I was proud of Ralph's plucky spirit. I'd worked hard to get him to that point, and it was quite a contrast to his former behavior.

He had first entered my kennel twelve weeks before, in the arms of his owner, Mrs. Jensen. Every hair on his body seemed to quiver in fright as the woman explained the reasons for which she had come.

"I already had two dogs before I acquired Ralph," she said. "Mutt and Jeff are very outgoing and full of mischief. I had gotten Ralph because I thought they would like another dog to play with."

"How do the other dogs react to Ralph?" I asked.

"Well, Mutt and Jeff have always loved to roughhouse with each other. Since Ralph has come into the picture, they team up and pounce on him every chance they get. Ralph is so afraid of them now that he spends most of his time in my bedroom—*under* the bed. He won't even come out to eat. I have to place his food under the bed for him. I have tried to get him accustomed to the rest of the house and to the other dogs, but as soon as I take him out and let him go, he scurries right back into my bedroom. I've never had a dog that has done that before. I don't know what to do."

Mrs. Jensen had pinpointed the problem. Ralph was much too sensitive to be jostled and bullied by the other two dogs. He was at the bottom of the pecking order and his only refuge was under his owner's bed. I explained this to Mrs. Jensen and advised her to find a home for Ralph with no other dogs for him to compete with.

"Oh dear," she said frowning. "I didn't want to give him away. I love all three of my dogs. Can't you teach him not to be afraid of the other dogs?"

I thought for a moment. "Well, I could possibly build up his self-image, if that is what you mean. It might take some doing, but it is a feasible alternative to giving him away."

"When can he start?" she said without hesitation.

I began Ralph's training with a relaxed, unpressured program to get him accustomed to the newness of his situation. I would walk him around the ring, whistling and talking to him until he finally relaxed. Once we had established a master-dog relationship through basic obedience, Ralph became more secure within himself, and his constant apprehension of being ambushed, eventually faded. Now he was ready for his image-building course.

I pondered how best to go about this next stage. It was going to be a delicate process to be sure. I had to set up a foolproof situation in which Ralph would have the upper hand. I decided to begin by using the ducks that I keep for retriever training. I let them out of their pen and went back to the kennel for Ralph.

The ducks were milling around the yard as we approached. Ralph was reluctant to get near them until he saw that they would waddle away if we came too close. Soon we were chasing them all over the yard. Ralph thought it was great fun to have something run from *him* for a change. Within three days, Ralph was eagerly anticipating our duck chases.

In order to broaden his experience, I set about walking him through our open fields where I train pheasant dogs, hoping to find a sitting jack rabbit to chase. I finally spotted one, laying low in a clump of grass. Ears down, the rabbit was as still as a statue. We crept closer, then suddenly charged. The jack rabbit darted out of its spot and bounded across the field with us in hot pursuit. We were no match for the rabbit's swiftness, of course, but the chase did wonders for Ralph's ego. He barked excitedly at the rapidly disappearing form. Everyday thereafter, when our basic obedience sessions were over, Ralph and I would chase all the jack rabbits out of the fields.

I devised a somewhat more elaborate scheme to extend Ralph's confidence around other dogs. I used a Labrador Retriever that I had been training for duck-work. I took the Lab out and gave her a *sit-stay* command at one end of the training ring. Next I placed a retrieving bumper behind her back at the opposite end of the training ring. Then I brought Ralph out. When we came within twenty feet of the Lab, Ralph let out a surprised bark. I immediately gave the Lab a hand signal for "back." When the Lab turned and ran back for the bumper, it appeared as though Ralph had chased her off. I reinforced the illusion by trotting after the retreating dog with Ralph running alongside of me. When the Lab picked up the bumper and turned to bring it to me, I had to stop her quickly with a sharp blast on my field whistle so that it wouldn't appear that she was coming after Ralph. She sat holding the bumper and I gave her a *stay* hand signal. Ralph must have felt ten feet tall. As I picked up the "conquering hero" and carried him away from the other dog, he looked back at the Lab and gave a final indignant bark.

After the episode with the Lab, Ralph was starting to feel his muscles. He would boldly investigate other dogs as we walked past their runs, and sometimes even bark at them. Ralph, although friendly and affectionate, was no longer the meek and mild-mannered dog he once had been. I felt a suitable nickname was in order, and decided upon "Tiger."

The transfer sessions with Mrs. Jensen went smoothly. She was extremely pleased with her little dog and she even liked his new name. I asked her to bring Mutt and Jeff along when she came for the last session. Ralph was going to have to confront these two, and I wanted to be on hand when he did. It was going to be Ralph's supreme test, for up to that point, all his "conquests" had been imaginary ones.

Mutt and Jeff were waiting in the car, and after the session was over, we took him out for the confrontation. The two dogs barked and wagged their tails excitedly when they saw good ol' Ralph coming. Life had probably been pretty dull without him. They watched from the rear platform area of the station wagon as I opened the back door and gave Ralph the "kennel" (which means "in") command. He jumped up on the back seat and I closed the door. That was Mutt and Jeff's cue. They came flying over the backrest and landed on Ralph. Mutt pinned him down and quickly grabbed an ear, while Jeff took hold of Ralph's tail and began to tug on it. The two dogs were really getting down to business when Ralph exploded out from under Mutt, bowling him over. Before Mutt could recover, he found himself on his back, with Ralph standing over him growling meancingly. Jeff, startled at the sudden reversal, had let go of Ralphs tail and jumped back over the backrest to "safety." Mutt was too surprised to do anything but submit to Ralph.

I waited a couple minutes for Ralph to establish, beyond any doubt, who would be number one from now on. Then I stuck my head through the open window. "Okay Ralph, that will do." He looked up at

MUTT WAS TOO SUPRISED TO DO ANYTHING BUT
SUBMIT TO RALPH...

me and wagged his tail. Mutt seized the opportunity to disengage himself and fly over the backrest to join Jeff.

There was something almost majestic in the way Ralph looked, sitting there with the whole back seat all to himself. I felt sure he'd never abuse his new-found strength by bullying Mutt and Jeff. But he had made it clear, they wouldn't have Ralph to pick on anymore.

I have found that by developing the mental discipline
of a problem dog through basic training alone, 85%
of its problems will disappear, without my working
on them directly.

Memories

"Good morning, Meisterfeld Ranch Kennels," I said answering the phone.

"Hello, this is Mr. Fieldstone. I have a question about my dog and I was hoping I could get your opinion on it."

"I'll do my best," I said, "although I prefer to see the dog. It's pretty difficult for me to get a clear picture of the situation over the phone."

"Well this has to do with an incident that happened last month. I have a two-year-old Dachshund whom I take for a walk every evening on a regular route. I guess some new people had moved into one of the houses along the way because this big dog I had never seen before, rushed out and attacked my dog. My dog was hurt pretty badly, but he is all right now. I had him at the veterinarians yesterday to have the stitches removed, so I asked the doctor if he thought my dog would remember what happpened to him and be afraid to walk by that house again. He told me that dogs have very short memories and that they do not retain negative experiences for very long. That is what I wanted to ask you about. *Will* my dog remember if I take him past that house again?"

"Well, Mr. Fieldstone, I can't say for sure how your dog will react in that situation. As far as the question of dogs having memories, I'll tell you about a sixteen-month-old Great Dane who was brought to me because he feared the new swimming pool his owners had installed. This dog refused to get any closer to it than twenty-five feet. He nearly pushed Lori, his owner, through a plate glass sliding door trying to get away when she attempted to introduce him to the water. Lori called the breeder to ask him about it and she learned that the dog had fallen into a swimming pool when he was only eight weeks old. There was no one home at the time and he wore his nails down to bloody stumps trying to climb out the side of the pool. Finally, the breeder returned and saved the pup. Time had not cured the dog's fear or erased the memory of the event.

"I also had a Brittany Spaniel who, after once finding the seven birds I had planted in the field, would remember where each one was the next day. I had to relocate the birds every day to make her hunt for them." I began to warm to the subject.

"As a matter of fact, many of my clients who have brought their dogs back after a year or more, tell me that as they turn the corner a mile away from the kennel, their dogs will suddenly become quiet. Some dogs react differently though. Karen, who owns a Keeshond, told me her dog gets all excited when he realizes he is coming to my kennel. Yet when she takes him to the veterinarian, he sulks.

"Retrievers that come back for brush-up training, even if they haven't been worked or hunted in the field for over a year, will usually recall all their commands after only one brush-up session." There was no stopping me now.

"Then there was the gentleman from Santa Rosa who drove by every Sunday for several weeks after I had trained his dog. I finally called him up out of curiosity. He said that he hadn't had time to work his dog, so he drove past the kennel once a week. 'It's amazing how my dog quiets down and behaves after going past your place,' he said. 'Lasts for four or five days.' "

I laughed self-consciously. "I didn't mean to be long winded, Mr. Fieldstone. But I leave it to you to decide whether dogs have memories or not. What do you think?"

"I think I'm going to take another route from now on," he said. "Thank you, Mr. Meisterfeld, you have been a help."

HER DOG GETS ALL EXCITED WHEN HE REALIZES
HE'S COMING TO MY KENNEL.....

Sean

Gladys Brown and I walked up and down the residential and city streets of Petaluma, hunting. Sean, her sleek, red Irish Setter trotted by her side. It was to be our last session after completing Sean's training. The purpose of our hunt that day was to find another dog so that Gladys could exercise her newly acquired control over Sean.

Gladys, a serenly beautiful woman with penetrating blue eyes, had brought Sean to me for a problem which had gotten out of control. She explained in her lilting Maryland accent how the dog had come to her at a particularly dark time in her life due to the passing on of her beloved husband. Sean was like a ray of light to her, and he had no trouble settling into his role as a companion.

As time went on, an exceptionally close bond had grown between them; so close in fact that Sean began to get possessive with Gladys and would protect her jealously. Sean loved women (still does) but he seemed to think that men and dogs posed a threat, and he wouldn't hesitate to challenge them if they invaded "his" personal territory. Consequently, Gladys had to be very selective as to where she walked him on public streets, avoiding potentially difficult situations whenever possible.

Gladys realized the seriousness of her predicament one day when Sean would not permit a young college student to visit his fiancee, who had moved in with Gladys. The new member of the household was officially under Sean's "protection."

Sean was an exceptionally strong-willed, intelligent and high-spirited dog. With his keen sense perception he was attempting to replace the man in the house; to fill a void in a devotional, servitude way.

After we talked at length, Gladys decided to leave Sean for training. . .

Although we couldn't seem to locate any dogs as we roamed the streets, there were ample opportunities to test Sean with the male pedestrians that passed by. I walked to the right of Gladys so that Sean, heeling on her left, would come close to the men as they passed. Sean was behaving beautifully, showing no concern as the strangers came near. But what we really needed was to test him on some strange dogs.

We had been searching for about two hours and were about to give up when I spotted a large, jet-black dog in the distance. It looked like it was heading in our direction. We had talked earlier about fear and we both agreed with the poet, Khalil Gibran: *"And if it is fear you would dispel, the seat of that fear is in your heart and not in the hand of the feared."* Now it looked as though this belief was about to be put to the test.

I could tell that Gladys hadn't seen it yet, so I quickly reminded her of Sean's special commands; "be good" which was to be used about twenty feet away, "leave it" if he showed *any* interest in the other dog, and ultimately "nein" which is used for correction. Just as I finished talking, Gladys saw the dog. It was a huge Great Dane, a male. He was half a block away and coming toward us.

"Keep going straight ahead," I told her. "You're in control now." With that I took off across the street to leave her on her own.

The suddeness of my departure must have been frightening to her. She paused uncertainly for a moment, then like the determined Taurus she is, turned to meet the other dog.

The Great Dane saw Sean and raised his tail in a challenge. Sean saw him too and Gladys gave him the "be good" command. The gap was closing and the Great Dane was primed for a fight as he eye-balled Sean. I heard Gladys say "leave it" and Sean turned his head to her. Gladys kept walking as the Great Dane came up to Sean's left side and gave him the sniff test. Sean kept his head riveted toward Gladys. Without his challenge returned, the Great Dane quickly lost interest and went on his way. The whole scene was less than a couple of minutes, but it seemed like hours to me, and most probably a lifetime to Gladys.

I returned to them and I could see the sparkling light of triumph in her eyes. I didn't know it then, but a dramatic change had just taken place in Gladys. She wrote me a letter after taking Sean home that says it all:

"Bill, you might be greatly surprised and perhaps astounded at what I am about to say. Since my good husband's passing, I have been wandering around in, let's say a "fog." I used to be a very active and alive person.

Since my visits to your kennel with my dog (notice I said dog and not lover) I have learned a great deal from you; your patience and understanding, not only for my dog but for me as well. (I might add, I miss the visits very much)

You are responsible for my going back to reading (self-help books) I have also registered at College of Marin for several classes, am entertaining more at home and "looking around." I have actually come out of my shell and started to live again.
The Friday morning we walked and walked to find a dog to dismiss my fears, did more than dismiss my fears; I actually found myself once again that morning. Thank You."

Since Sean's training, Gladys has moved back to Maryland where she is now an accomplished artist and author of the book, *Sean: my pal.**

Through the years, many of my clients have told me how much they have learned about themselves through their dogs. But my encounter with Gladys and Sean remains one of the warmest highlights of my career. I learned that an awakening isn't always a thunder-and-lightening experience. Sometimes it can be as simple and poignant as walking through the streets, looking for a dog. . . .

*Published by—5 Senses
Box 12 A
Huntingtown, MD 20639

For You I Pine

There are many things that make up a rewarding day for me: a satisfied client taking his dog home; a whole day of training dogs without *one* "accident" in the training ring (very distracting); a person asking me for advice—and actually taking it! Then there will always be those "other" days when things don't necessarily go wrong, but they don't exactly go right either.

One such time involved a sweet-faced Cocker Spaniel of questionable upbringing. Her owner, Mr. Smythe, had obtained her from the San Francisco S.P.C.A. and later brought her to me when a problem had developed.

"When I leave for work my neighbors tell me that Rosebud cries and whines for hours. I've tried alot of things to get her to stop this nonsense." He gave Rosebud a look of mock severity that sent a quiver of delight through her. She rolled her alluring brown eyes up at him. Mr. Smythe was a small, frail looking fellow with a worried expression that never left him—even when he smiled. But to Rosebud, he was adorable.

"You are my last resort, so-to-speak," he continued. "I own my own home at present, but this fall I'm moving to Southern California where I have an option on an apartment. You can understand why I can't have this problem in an apartment building."

"Absolutely," I agreed.

"I've tried so *many* things to break her of it but so far nothing has worked. Someone said to breed her so I did. She had five puppies, only she'd rather abandon them to be with me. I finally had to enclose her in a pen to keep her with them until they were old enough to place in homes.

"Then I took someone else's advice and had her spayed thinking that would help—it didn't. Mr. Meisterfeld, I don't mind telling you, I was really in a dither over this. But I wasn't so desperate as to grab the

129

next piece of advice, which was to get her a companion-playmate so she wouldn't be lonely when I'm gone. I figured if her pups couldn't satisfy her, then why should another dog? Unless she wanted a dog more her own age to play with. Then again, I didn't want to get another dog only to learn that *that* wasn't the answer either." He ran a bony hand through his thin hair.

"Just by luck a friend of mine was going on vacation and asked if I could take care of Hans, his German Shepherd, for two weeks. Hans and Rosebud were friends so I said I would. I thought it would be the perfect opportunity to test out the latest theory. Well she and Hans got along just fine at home. It looked like maybe that was the answer after all. But just to really put it to the test, I decided to leave them alone and see what would happen. Very quietly, I sneaked out to the garage, but before I could even open my car door, I heard Rosie's whine coming from inside the house. I tell you, I couldn't believe it. It got louder and louder until after about five minutes you could hear her a block away. And if *that* wasn't bad enough, Hans picked up the habit from Rosie. When my friend finally came back, all he could say was, 'Thanks alot!' " The poor man looked distraught.

"What you've told me so far has been very helpful, Mr. Smythe. But I'm sure I'll be able to tell you more after I work with Rosebud for a few hours. When you come back I can tell you what I've found and possibly suggest a solution to your problem."

"I would be most grateful," he said.

And so Rosebud was left with me for evaluation. I got right to work so as to have all my tests done before Mr. Smythe returned. There were several things that might be prompting Rosebud to pine away in her owner's absense. I wanted to test her sensitivity, fears, temperament, attention span and, most important, willingness to serve and please. She knew all the basic obedience commands and accepted my handling well. All other aspects checked out normal. Without her owner's main complaint of whining and howling when left alone, I could not fault her. Compared to most of the dogs that I encounter, Rosebud was very well balanced.

Mr. Smythe was not due back for another hour, so I decided to leave Rosebud alone in her run until then and see how she acted. She didn't make a sound. This was particularly significant, in that it told me the cause was *not* with the dog but with the relationship.

As the time drew near for Mr. Smythe to return, Rosebud demonstrated a very high sense perception. She seemed to know just when her owner was coming. I happened to notice his car approaching from half a mile away. At the same time Rosebud began a low

MR. SMYTHE DIDN'T REALLY HEAR ME·····

whine, which increased to a demanding bark as he pulled into the driveway and parked his car. I retrieved Rosebud from her run and met Mr. Smythe in my office to discuss what I had found.

"Well, Mr. Smythe, she is a beautifully balanced dog." He looked surprised. "Can you tell me just a little more about her?"

"My goodness," he said. "I thought I'd covered everything. What else would you like to know?"

"What, for instance, do *you* do with Rosebud when you're home?" The man looked puzzled.

"Beg your pardon?"

"I mean, do you play with her alot? Is she right with you *all* the time?"

"Yes. I try to give her enough attention when I'm home. She has lots of toys, but she'll only play with them if I toss them for her. She loves that. All the rest of the time she's right at my feet. I can't even go to the bathroom without her carrying on outside. She's so persistent that I have to give in and open the door. I even let her sleep on my bed at night, because she cries if I leave her downstairs."

"We all have a tendency to develop a togetherness with our dogs, however there should be times and places when your life is separate; *especially* when you want to shave or . . ." I paused groping for the right words.

"Yes, I get the drift," he said, and laughed nervously.

"I do believe you have a good dog here, but she has been manipulating you, *with your help.* You need to stop catering to her emotionally. You have to let her know who is boss and what is expected of her. An emotional tie as strong as this cannot just happen. It took time to develop and it will take time to change it."

I outlined a program for him to follow at home, designed to break the cycle. "I'm sure that you'll be able to work this out yourself, Mr. Smythe. Just remember that the emotional dependency has to be cut by you. Be firm."

"Thank you Mr. Meisterfeld, I appreciate all that you've told me." he said shaking my hand. With that he tenderly gathered his dog up into his arms and left with Rosebud licking his face appreciatively.

I shook my head slowly and let out a sigh. Apparently Mr. Smythe hadn't really heard me. Didn't I make myself clear? Oh well, I thought, I hope everything works out for him. But, that's the way it goes in this business; win some, lose some. I had done my best.

Goliath

I wondered what might have gone wrong with Goliath. Diana hadn't said over the phone, although I could tell she was upset. But I would find out soon enough because she was due at any moment. As I waited for her, I thought back to the first time she'd brought her 150-pound Old English Sheepdog in for training.

"I do hope he'll be alright." Diana said to me after I'd put the dog in the run.

I smiled. "Oh, don't worry about *him*. The question is, are *you* going to be alright?"

Diana laughed. "Well, I have to admit that I'll probably miss him, even if he *is* a pain in the you-know-what most of the time. But I'm grateful that you're going to teach him some manners for me. I don't know why he loves to chase people on bicycles like he does." Diana raised her skirt slightly, revealing skinned and bandaged knees. "I can't take any more of this. He drags me around on the leash like a rag doll. Maybe if he didn't outweigh me by forty-five pounds I could handle him. But as it is, I'm bruised and sore in places I never knew I had before. I'm afraid to let go because he might run off and not come back or something."

"Does he give your husband the same trouble?"

"No, my husband has very little time for him actually. Oh, he romps with Goliath when he gets a chance and isn't too tired. But that's about all. The two boys play with him too—when they're around. You know how teenagers are; to them home is just a pit-stop. They come in, refuel, maybe rest, then they're off again." Diana shrugged her shoulders and smiled. "So it's just Goliath and me, mainly. That's why I had to think of someway for me to control him. And that's why I'm here."

Goliath's initial training had proved to be highly successful. I remembered how happy Diana was when the time came for her to take him home.

"There are three things that you're going to have to watch with him," I had told her in the last training session. "Number one, Goliath has a strong will-to-power and is aggressive by his own nature. Number two, you have to maintain the master-dog* relationship we have now established; that means correcting him the *first* time he attempts any old behavior pattern. Number three, you cannot use him for an emotional substitute."

Diana understood.

"And remember, if you have any questions later on, don't hesitate to call." She said that she would.

Diana pulled into the parking lot of the kennel and soon she was sitting once again in my office with Goliath. I looked down at him and shook my head. He looked terrible. He had a wild, unfocused look in his eyes, which shifted nervously about the room. He was panting heavily and his tongue lolled out the side of his mouth.

"What's been happening since he left here?"

Diana shifted uneasily in her chair. She swallowed hard and from beginning to end, told me the whole story. . .

"When I drove home after our last session together, I was so thrilled about having a trained, obedient dog. In fact, I tried to remember everything you told me during our sessions so that I wouldn't make any mistakes in handling him. The next morning, before the rest of the family dispersed, I demonstrated the things Goliath and I had learned. Jim and the boys thought it was great. I was so proud!

"That afternoon as I got ready to take Goliath for a walk, I decided to go by way of the bicycle route. That's the one place I never dared take him before and I was a little scared. There were no bikes in sight as we approached the path, and I was grateful for that. After awhile I spotted a bicycle approaching in the distance. Goliath saw it too. Just as it whirred past, Goliath made a lunge for it. I said, 'NEIN,' and jerked on the leash as hard as I could. That surprised him, I think, because he got back into the heel position right away. I was shaking slightly but I realized that I had actually stopped him. The next time a bicycle approached, he checked with me before responding to it. I made it clear that he was to leave it alone, and he did. By the end of our walk I didn't even have to warn him to behave when a bike when by. In a couple of weeks, he'd lost interest in them altogether.

*How's & Why's of Psychological Dog Training

"He never got over his love of sprawling all over the furniture though. I gave him a special bed in one corner of the living room, but he didn't seem to like it. I caught him up on the couch several times with the boys, even though they knew I didn't want him up there. But he always got down when I told him to. Then the boys would start in. 'Aw, Mom, he's not hurting anything.' Well, after going through this so many times, my resistance began to crumble. Goliath had been so well-behaved in every other way, that as a reward I finally let him up on the couch. He seemed to be content with that for awhile, but then started to beg to get up on our bed. Before I knew it he was up on the furniture all the time. But . . . I let it go," she said wistfully.

"One day I noticed that Goliath had gotten very interested in motorcycles. He'd sit at the front room window watching for them to come by so he could bark at them. I felt uneasy about that but I couldn't get him to stop. I should have called you about it, but I thought I could work it out somehow. I was very careful walking him and if I heard a motorcycle coming, I would try to avoid it by stepping off onto a side street or something. But one day I let my mind drift and didn't hear the motorcycle through the usual traffic sounds. It came up behind us and before I knew it, I was on the ground. Goliath dragged me right out into the street. I was terrified and tried to let go of his leash but my hand was completely through the loop. I thought I was good as dead because the cars were zooming past, honking their horns. A young man walking by saw me and ran to help. He caught Goliath and helped me to the sidewalk. That was the last time I ever walked him. I left him out in our small backyard from then on.

"After that episode, I decided to go back to the old rules, but Goliath no longer obeyed me. It wasn't that he questioned my authority, he ignored it completely. But I perservered, hoping I would regain control if I worked him faithfully. Still, he refused to get off the furniture ever since I'd told him it was okay.

"One night I made his food and gave it to him. I went through the whole routine of making him sit and stay until I said it was okay for him to eat. Well, he dug in as he always does, and I noticed that the food was starting to spill out over the side of the dish, so I went and got a newspaper to put underneath it. As I got near him I heard a deep growl. Goliath had his head low to the dish and he was staring at me. He growled again to let me know he meant business. I called Jeff over and asked him to walk slowly toward Goliath. The dog growled at him too. He became increasingly intolerant of us when he was eating, until we couldn't get within ten feet of him. Finally I'd mix his food, put it in the laundry room, shove Goliath in after it and shut the door until he was finished.

"My breaking point came one hot afternoon. I was planning a small dinner party for that evening and was cleaning up the house. When I went to start on our bedroom, I found Goliath sprawled out on the bed. I told him to get down but he just raised up and looked at me. It seemed like all the frustration and worry he'd caused me surfaced at that moment. I was tired of playing games with him; tired of letting him manipulate me. It was hot, I was in a hurry, and I was angry. I went for his collar to pull him off the bed, and without warning he snapped at me. He bit my hand, but not seriously. It scared me to think he would actually do it. I realized then that he wasn't going to get any better. That's when I called you." Diana looked at me hopefully. "Is there any way you can get him leveled off again?"

It's not uncommon for my clients to ease up on their dog's discipline after they've had them home for a while. Most dogs can handle it pretty well without taking advantage of their added privileges. But in Goliath's case, it was a disaster. I needed time to find out just what it would take to straighten him out again.

"Why don't you leave Goliath here, then call me tomorrow morning. I'd like to see how much training he's retained, and also check him at feeding time before I give you a definite answer."

The next morning, Diana called exactly at nine. I was ready for her.

"Diana, I've never seen a dog regress as drastically as this one has," I said after she asked me what I'd found. "He even seems to be having memory lapses. I don't think he can be trusted any more."

"B-but what should I do?"

"Well, as he is now, I would advise you to have him put to sleep."

Diana was horrified. "Put him to sleep?" she said with a catch in her voice. "Can't you do *anything* for him? It's *my* fault he went backward, not his." She was making a great effort not to cry.

I wasn't sure Goliath could handle another reprogramming. Yet deep down I felt it might be possible—*if* Diana would maintain the training once I succeeded. I had to impress upon her the importance of discipline in Goliath's case.

"I'll tell you what," I said. "I'll take him for training again. But I'm going to have to lay down some conditions for you to follow this time. The first one is that you do *not* give in to his demands any more. I also want your husband and sons in on the training sessions. You're going to have to work together as a family to maintain his discipline. It's not going to be easy for him *or* me. He's nervous and unpredictable. But once I get him straightened out, it's up to you to keep him there. He'll never make it here a third time." I paused to let my words sink in. "Agreed?" I asked finally.

Diana let out a long sigh. "Agreed."

Goliath's retraining was a long and ardorous process. It was not just a matter of teaching him the commands all over again; he already knew them. I had to break through the mental "fog" Goliath seemed to be in. I taught him the special "leave-it" command to keep him out of immediate or potential trouble. This was for motorcycles, bicycles, other dogs, and people. I worked Goliath mostly in the city where he was subject to all his previous temptations. I also trained him to stop eating anytime I gave the "leave-it" command.

With his boundaries once again firmly established, and a solid master-dog relationship renewed, Goliath leveled off to the normal behavior he previously had. It took me longer to reprogram Goliath than it did to train him the first time. After he had left, I couldn't help wondering how he was getting along. Was Diana adhering to her part of the deal? My questions were answered several months later at Christmastime, when I received a card from Diana. She wrote:

> Dear Bill,
> You would not believe what a real pet Goliath has become. He still obeys all the commands you taught him. He really seems to want to please us. Thank you so much for helping us with his training.
> Merry Christmas. . .

..... MERRY CHRISTMAS!.....

A Smart "First Timer"

I've trained some wily dogs in my time. But I think the prize for the most resourceful dog should go to a German Shepherd that had been left with me for a weeks boarding. The owners were going on vacation and it was the first time the dog had ever been in a kennel or run.

I am always careful to observe these "first timers" when they're put in a run. Their foremost thoughts are usually of escape, and to prevent them from injuring themselves, it is necessary for me to discourage them right away. Although the runs are fully enclosed and covered, some dogs will actually climb the fence to try and get out the top of the run. Other dogs will try to chew holes in the fence. Still others will dash themselves bodily against the gate.

But this German Shepherd was in a class by himself. As I put him in his run I watched him watching me secure the gate with a safety lock. I left him and went across the yard to a storage building that has windows facing the kennel. I had a perfect view of all the runs from there.

After I was out of sight, the Shepherd stood up on his hind legs facing the gate. Keeping his balance by leaning his shoulder on the side of the run, he stuck both paws through the fence. Thus situated, he began to work at the top latch with one paw while trying to trip the safety latch with the other paw. He worked at it for several minutes then dropped down. I thought he'd given up, but after a short rest he was up and at it again.

Although he didn't succeed in tripping the latch, I went back and put a double lock on the gate. Who knows, with that kind of persistence, he just might have made it!

HE BEGAN WORK AT THE TOP LATCH...

Give Me That Old Soft Shoe

The piercing screem filled the air once again. I watched the young woman bend down to comfort and apologize to her Norwegian Elkhound for stepping on his paw for the umteenth time. I was conducting a psychological dog obedience class and these regular outbursts were beginning to have a disruptive effect on the other dogs.

This scene seemed to repeat itself four or five times during each class period. I suspected something peculiar was going on so I observed the young woman closely. After calling for the class to halt, I saw the Elkhound slide his paw right under his owner's foot just as she stepped down, setting the whole process in motion again.

"Susan," I said, "would you like to stop that once and for all?"

She blushed, embarrassed. "I sure would. But I guess I'm just too clumsy. I keep stepping all over him."

I then explained how the dog had been manipulating her for attention. "The next time he does that, step down hard; and don't apologize. Totally disregard him."

Susan followed my advice when the next opportunity arose. The dog let out an extra loud yelp, but Susan ignored him. I'm sure the dog's pride hurt worse than his paw, and for the remaining six weeks of the class, it never happened again.

THE DOG LET OUT AN EXTRA LOUD YELP, BUT SUSAN
IGNORED HIM.....

Mother, May I?

There has been quite a bit of study on dog behavior in recent years, and it is generally accepted that dogs do not learn by observation (or imitation, if you will). That is, a dog will not learn to perform an act by watching another dog doing it. There are those, however, who do not necessarily agree with this, and I am one of them. My view stems from an experience I'd had many years ago with Point, my German Shorthaired Pointer, and has since been substantiated by my experiences with other dogs over the years.

I was building a house on the East bank of the Vermillion River back in Ohio, and also getting Baroness (Point's mother) ready for the National Retriever Championship. It was May, and the winter ice and snow had melted and combined with the spring rains, making the river current swift.

I stood on an embankment 25 feet from the water's edge and threw a retrieving bumper into the water. KERSPLASH! It landed about 150 feet from the river bank where it was immediately seized by the current. I looked down at Baroness, waiting eagerly for my cue.

"Fetch!" My command sent her running down the embankment and, with a powerful leap, into the icy-cold water. The bumper had traveled a good distance downstream, but Baroness had little difficulty overtaking it. Once she had secured the bumper in her mouth, she turned around, swam upstream until she reached the spot where she had entered the water, trotted up the embankment and sat in front of me. "Give." She released the bumper into my hand.

"Okay, shake," I said, and she sent a shower of water flying. This is something I teach all water dogs. It allows the handler to get out of the way so as to keep dry; but, more important, it prevents the dog from dropping the bird to shake, which could allow a stunned or crippled bird to possibly get away.

POINT WATCHED HIS MOTHER'S WORKOUTS WITH INTEREST...

I was preparing to give Baroness another retrieve when I heard Point barking again. The kennel where I kept my dogs was situated next to the house on a sloping hill about 75 feet from where Baroness and I stood. Point, just shy of a year old, had been watching his mother's workouts with interest since he was a pup. I had plans of training Point to eventually follow in his mother's footsteps. He had a lot of good qualities, but at that time he had only basic obedience training. I felt there was no rush to get him up to Baroness' level of performance. But Point was less patient than I. By his insistant barking, I knew that he wanted to do some water retrieving too. I could just picture him trying to retrieve a bumper for the first time without any preparation for it. If the cold, swift water didn't send him shivering back to me, he would probably lose the bumper downstream.

This of course is not the best way to introduce young dogs to their first water retrieve. Better to let them develop their swimming abilities first. Most will find themselves working their front paws above the water's surface, resulting in much splashing. The splashing in turn hinders their vision and causes them to lose sight of the bumper. Or, as so often happens, their flailing paws make contact with the bumper and inadvertantly push it under the water, and it might pop up behind them. All in all, it can be very confusing to an inexperienced dog. But how can you warn an aspiring young retriever about the pitfalls? There's only one way.

Okay, I thought. I'll let him do it *once*. When he finds out how hard it really is, he'll be happy just to watch until I'm ready to teach him.

I took Point out of the kennel and brought him down to our practice site. I kept Baroness close by as a reliable back-up. No sense losing good equipment to Lake Erie. I gave Point a sit-stay on top of the river bank, then tossed out a bumper. KERSPLASH! It too landed about 150 feet from the bank. Point held his stay. "Fetch," I commanded, and off he went. I was surprised to see him take a flying leap into the water, and watched very closely when he hit for any signs of shyness, fear or panic. But Point leveled off immediately and demonstrated his mother's style of keeping his front paws low in the water for more powerful movement. Head low, eyes fixed on the elusive bumper, he quickly closed the gap between himself and the bumper.

Point made a 180-degree arc, stopped paddling long enough to grab the bumper without disturbing the water, then (wonders!) headed back to me, instead of making for the nearest shore. He swam to the area where he entered the water, splashed up the bank, sat

facing me and waited until I gave the release word. I took the bumper and he shook. It was an excellent performance. The only thing he didn't do was wait for my permission to shake.

"Well, smarty," I said. "Since you seem to know what you're doing, let's see how you do on a *double* retrieve." Point wagged his stub of a tail enthusiastically.

In order not to make this maneuver too difficult or confusing, I threw the bumpers closer to shore to avoid the main current. I fired a shot from my blank pistol and tossed bumper number one to my left. I fired again and threw bumper number two to my right. I gave the fetch command. Without hesitation, Point took off for the last drop, which was the right thing to do on a double retrieve. The last gets picked up first and vice versa.

By the time he reached bumper number two, the current had caught it and carried it approximately 100 feet downstream. Point made the pick-up in the characteristic arc, then headed upstream. As he was coming in, bumper number one drifted past him, about 25 feet away, closer to the main current. Point made no attempt to change course and go after it, but he did appear to mark the direction in which it was going. He returned within ten feet of where he entered the water and delivered the bumper to me. I gave him a second fetch command and he was off again.

By now bumper number one was over 300 feet away and heading for the bend in the river. It would be a difficult retrieve even for a seasoned dog, let alone an inexperienced one. I was certain that in my enthusiasm I had given him more than he could handle.

Point was on course and he reached the bumper just as it started to disappear around the bend. Once again he picked up the bumper on a turn and headed back to me. Now he was in the main current trying to swim directly against it. This is much different from swimming *with* the current, or in the outer edges. To be able to make headway required more powerful strokes than Point was capable of. Neither did he have the experience of Baroness to angle out of the main flow. In a few minutes Point was pushed back 50 feet or more down river, while he struggled harder and harder.

I was about to jump in my boat and pick him up when an idea struck me. If he could only take a directional control signal, I would be able to maneuver him to the river bank and to safety. I gave three short blasts on my training whistle and extended my right arm to signal a 90-degree right turn (which would have Point turning to his left). The sound of the whistle was shrill and effective. Point made a sharp-angle turn and went for shore. He pulled himself out of the water, climbed the bank and walked tiredly up the road to where Baroness and I waited.

Point presented the bumper to me with weary pride. He seemed to know he had just accomplished something extraordinary. I was proud too, and grateful that in spite of his difficulties, his interest in retrieving was still intact. I took him back to his run where he slept for the rest of the day in his favorite spot—on *top* of his doghouse.

It's true that some dogs will instinctively retrieve without any training whatsoever. But how did Point know he was supposed to exit the water at the same spot he had entered it? Or what the whistle and hand signals meant? Or which bumper to pick up first on a double retrieve? He could not have performed all the finer aspects of the exercise through instinct alone. I can only surmise that he learned by observing his mother's daily workouts.

Of course, one may call this only an isolated incident. That might be true if not for the fact that, without further training, Point took first place in the German Shorthaired Pointer Retriever Trial (puppy class) the following week. He made a believer out of *me!*

No Strings Attached

Mrs. Caramy had sought my help when she had run into some difficulty in training her four-month-old Cocker Spaniel.

"Corky will do a *sit* as long as I'm holding the leash," she explained. "But if I tell him to *stay,* and walk away, he won't sit any longer than half a minute."

It sounded like an easy enough problem to solve, so I suggested she bring Corky in for one training session, which was probably all the training he would need.

During our session, we tried several corrective methods to get Corky to *sit-stay,* all of which failed to produce the desired results. He was a smart little dog and always seemed to figure out ahead of time what we were up to.

"I think we are just going to have to outsmart him," I said. "Why don't you take Corky outside for a walk, Mrs. Caramy, while I get set up in here. I don't want him to see what I'm doing this time."

After she and the dog had gone outside, I took a 75 foot check cord and threw it over one of the 12 foot-high rafters. I arranged the cord so that the end with the snap on it hung down against one wall and stopped about three feet from the floor of the training ring. I threaded the other end of the cord through a window on the opposite wall. Below the window was a knothole. I went outside and explained my plan to Mrs. Caramy:

"I want you to walk Corky around the ring and stop exactly where the drop cord is hanging down by the wall. Give him a *sit-stay,* and very discreetly hook the loop end of the leash to the snap, then walk away. I'm going to be outside watching through a knothole. When I see Corky get up, I'll pull on the check cord, and just when you see the leash go up, give the verbal correction. That way it will seem like the correction is coming out of nowhere, and he might think twice before attempting to break a *sit-stay* again." She liked my plan.

HIS GAZE RESTED DIRECTLY ON THE KNOTHOLE!...

I took my position outside and she went through the steps I had outlined. When she walked away from the dog, he seemed to sense something was wrong. Instead of getting up as he had been doing, he looked around and noticed the check cord. To my amazement, Corky followed the check cord with his eyes, up the wall to the rafter, across to the window and down where his gaze rested directly on the knothole. He stared intently right into my eye, then turned away to watch his owner. He didn't break his command.

My elaborate scheme had worked, although not in the way I had planned. Corky would not give me that satisfaction.

Patches

by Claude Spitzer

When I was thirteen years old, I lived in Monterey, California. As a child I often yearned for a pet to call my own. I brought home lizards, frogs and even a bird I managed to catch. At first I was content with these new friends, but I would inevitably release them. Either I realized I didn't know how to care for them and let them go, or I felt they desperately wanted to get back to their natural environment. I felt happy for them in that respect, but very sad that they were no longer mine. We had some chickens for pets, but they offered little pleasure for me. I couldn't catch or pet them, so they couldn't really be my friends either.

One day a friend of ours stopped by with his dog, which he could no longer keep, and gave him to us. He was a friendly old dog and he took to me like weeds in a garden. We had great times together, and he followed me everywhere I went. I found out, to my delight, that he could even do tricks like rolling over and shaking hands. We were the greatest of buddies—for one week. Then my mother came to me and told me the terrible news; we had to give the dog away. We couldn't afford to keep him because we were poor. So, we drove to Castroville to a big farmhouse, and there we traded the dog for two crates of artichokes. I can still recall how awful I felt. Artichokes were a poor substitute for my dog—how could I love artichokes? The heartbreak stayed with me for a long time. I even promised myself I would never again have a dog, for fear of having to give it up. I didn't feel I could endure another separation from a pet I had grown to love.

Not until twenty years later did I get involved with another dog. Having a love for the outdoors, especially for hunting and fishing, I attended a film on hunting pheasants with dogs. I was impressed, not so much with how well the dogs performed, but with how they related to their masters. It looked as though the dogs enjoyed being told what to do, which I could not understand. With my limited knowledge of dogs at the time, I felt that a happy dog was one who did what *it* wanted to do—not what the owner might want it to do. Later, I was to find out differently. But the stage was set; I decided to get a dog. I didn't know which breed I wanted, but I envisioned having a dog that would be both my personal pet and a good hunting companion.

I began to investigate all the facts and facets of hunting dogs. A Labrador Retriever would be too big for my home, and I didn't want a dog as small as a Beagle. I finally decided that I would get a Brittany Spaniel. They are medium-sized dogs which I thought to be beautiful, with their random coloring of liver and white.

I patiently waited, looking in newspaper ads, checking bulletin boards at work, and talking to people. Finally, one day I found an advertisement for Brittany Spaniel pups in Petaluma. I drove to the address and talked briefly with the owners, who said they used their dogs for deer hunting. They showed me the parents, and after seeing them, I knew this breed would be just right for me.

There were six pups fenced off from the parents and I sat down to observe them. I remembered reading that to select the best pup, one must look for two things: how healthy the pup is, and how it related to you. Well, they all looked healthy, and they were so similar that I had no way of keeping track of which was which. I asked for some masking tape, tore off six pieces and numbered them, then placed a number on each pup. I then sat back and observed how they related to each other. Some huddled together as though they were afraid to explore, while others ventured out bravely, looking like clumsy little clowns. I then took each pup away from its littermates to observe how it related to me. One or two came to me right away, and I reasoned that if they came to me that willingly, they might as easily go to anyone else. I didn't feel that was desirable, and ruled them out. Some pups, on the other hand, wouldn't have anything to do with me. But number five was different. She wanted to come to me, but was very tentative about it, and approached me with caution. I liked that. I knew I had to win the dog over, and that it would not run off with any stranger. It was ironic that this little puppy would act this way toward me, because I felt the same way when dealing with other people. Once the puppy overcame its initial shyness, it followed me everywhere I went. This was the one! On the way home I named her June, because it was the first day of June.

Everything had been prepared for our arrival at the house. I had bought her a bed, had newspapers laid on the kitchen floor, and I had used the tailgate of my truck to keep her off the livingroom carpet. When she cried from loneliness I would console her, something which, as time passed, became a problem. At first I didn't mind because I felt that she was just a lonely pup who needed some love, and I was more than willing to give it to her. But when I was occupied with other things, I would become upset with her when she began her ruckus. It had become a pattern for me to cater to her demands. I rationalized that all pups were like that and that I would just have to "grin and bear it." I was unaware that I should have been firm in establishing my role as master. I felt that in order for June to be free and happy, she should have what she wanted.

She became more and more of a nuisance, and neighbors began to complain about her incessant whining and barking. I felt that if I spent more time with her it might help, but it didn't. I hoped that her attitude would change as she grew older, that she would begin to mellow, but in the meantime it was difficult to cope with her. It all seemed worth it, however, in the few moments we were able to play, for I loved this dog and she filled my lonely hours. Not until later did I fully realize that June's problems were really *my* problems, and that I had created them in her. Compounding the problem were my feelings of anger and despair whenever I tried to demand obedience, and succeeded in making her fear me instead.

Once when I came home from work, she showed no desire to retrieve her bone, and when I insisted, she ran to the farthest corner of the yard. I didn't admit it then, but she was obviously resentful toward me. I began to seriously doubt whether she could ever hunt, or even have the desire to do so. I was unsure about how to handle the situation, so I backed off and did nothing.

I was relieved when June was one year old, since it was time for her training to begin, and when a friend recommended Bill Meisterfeld, I looked his phone number up in the yellow pages. Bill wanted to see June to determine if she could hunt. My friend drove up to Bill's kennels with us. When we arrived, Bill approached me and shook my hand. His handshake was very strong and his smile assured me. His expression and mannerisms made me feel that he would do a professional job in turning June into a good, obedient hunting dog—if she qualified.

While we talked, I noticed that the ranch had an aura of quiet peacefulness that amazed me. When I asked Bill about this, he replied that the dogs in the kennels didn't bark because they had been trained not to bark. I thought to myself, wouldn't it be great if June didn't yelp or bark for attention all the time?

As we continued to talk, he showed me around his kennels, but I was most impressed by the quietness. All I could hear were the sounds of birds chirping outside. "How could it be?" I wondered. "Did he use force to quiet them, or did he give them love or confidence to make them accept their environment?"

Bill requested that he have about four hours alone with June, so my friend and I left. I had a feeling that she could instinctively hunt, but would she be trainable? Those four hours seemed an eternity, and when we came back I could hardly wait to hear what Bill had found. He informed me that she was quite "birdie," and that she was neither gun-shy or man-shy. At that moment, I felt elated. There *was* hope for June! As Bill talked in his soft, positive voice, I decided to leave June there so he could begin training her. And I felt relieved that I could be free to do the things I wanted to do again, without being "hounded" and pestered by June. But, as the time went by, I also missed her. I began to realize that she had been serving a useful purpose in my life; she had been giving me the companionship I needed to keep from feeling lonely.

Now that I *was* alone, I began to have conflicting feelings about my decision. At times I wished she were back home; but then I'd think about how good it was going to feel to have an obedient, well-trained dog. With that, I was somewhat satisfied. But everyday when I came home from work and she wasn't there, that empty feeling came back, and I'd wish she were home again.

It was during these emotionally unsettled times that Bill called and informed me that June was almost uncontrollable. He sensed that there was some kind of extra-sensory perception going on between June and myself, and suggested that if she was to be rehabilitated, I would have to change some of my ways. He suggested that I not concern myself with her as much as possible, as it was affecting her training. And after all, *I* was paying for this. I began to look at the situation as an investment, and could see that the less involved I was, the less expensive it would be for me in the long run. I began to think more about other things, and the time began to fly by.

About thirteen weeks later, Bill phoned again and asked me if I wanted to see how June was progressing. I met him at the kennel, and when he first brought the dog out, she jumped all over me with excitement. But within a minute or two, she started sniffing and investigating the area around me. It seemed as though she no longer knew me. Bill explained that he had started to reprogram her emotionalism, and that at the completion of her training, she would be a good hunting dog. I felt good about the progress she was making, and began to envision myself and her, hunting pheasants together. I spent a lot of my time reading everything I could find on pheasant hunting. My dream was about to become a reality!

June's training was nearing completion when Bill called me in for a consultation. He didn't talk much about June, however; he wanted to talk about me. He said that in order for the positive changes in June's behavior to continue, I would have to treat her as a dog, not as a substitute for human companionship. I couldn't comprehend this at first, but I trusted Bill because I knew he cared about the dog, and I had faith in his experience. I decided to follow his suggestions completely.

When it was time for me to be trained as June's master, I learned that the past had to be forgotten. As the first step, Bill suggested I give June a new name. After much deliberation, I named her Patches. Now it really seemed as though June never existed. Here was this dog who resembled June, but who looked at me in a different way, a look that no longer said, "Do this for me." In its place there was an attentive look that said, "What do you want me to do?"

Bill began to show me how to handle Patches on the leash. I was flabbergasted at how well she did. Bill, in his quiet, strong way, demonstrated all the commands: heel, stay, ho, down and the rest. She did them perfectly. Now it was my turn. He emphasized again that I was the master and Patches was the servant-dog. I felt quite nervous and I sensed that Patches knew it also. She was confused when I took the leash because I was so emotional. I felt that I couldn't take over. I tried not to show my weakness as I went through the motions of working Patches, but I felt insecure and uncertain. I was glad when the session was over. I went home and thought about the whole episode to figure out why I felt the way I did. I finally blamed it on just being nervous, and tried to shrug it off.

The next session was almost a duplicate of the first, except that I was becoming more familiar with the routine, although I still didn't feel comfortable with the situation. It was then that Bill told me I could very easily cause Patches to revert to her former habits, which was what I feared. It began to dawn on me that *I* was the whole problem. He mentioned that there was going to be an introductory talk given at the PSI Center† in Oakland, dealing with self-awareness and positive change. He invited me to join him. I went home that day thinking about his offer and it began to trouble me. I asked myself questions like: what am I really doing? Do I deserve this dog? Can I measure up to being her master?

...WHETHER WE WALK, PLAY OR HUNT,
SHE IS A TRUE COMPANION·····

After I took Patches home, I devoted a half hour every day to working her on the leash. I demanded perfection from Patches and I looked for every flaw. I got angry when she faulted and would sometimes yell at her, which caused her to cower in fear of me. Bill had instructed me not to show anger, but at times I couldn't help it. I was really angry at myself, but only realized it after it happened.

As I begn to feel more comfortable with controlling her, I became the "new master" more and more. When I took her out in the field to practice with her, I gave her the "hie-on" command and she would immediately begin to hunt. It was beautiful to see her sweeping back and forth in front of me, and when she pointed for me for the first time, it was exhilarating. When I blew the whistle either two or three times, she would turn to the left or the right instantly. When she inadvertantly wandered too far ahead of me, all I had to do was give six or more short blasts on the whistle and she would come back. We worked out almost every day and I began to gain more confidence in myself. To see Patches do what Bill had trained her to do gave me great joy.

When I talked with Bill he continued to suggest that I take the course given by PSI, but I continued to procrastinate and say that I wasn't ready. I joined a pheasant-hunting club and when the season opened, I went to the club for the first time. I walked Patches on the leash as we approached the field. I released her and gave the "hie-on" command, and she began to hunt. Her eagerness and energy was simply amazing. Although we made no contact with any pheasants for an hour or so, I was in a state of wonderment. I could not believe her desire to please *me!* She loved to hunt for me, and I allowed her to do what she could do best. It was this that made me finally realize that *I* was not doing *my* best for myself. So, with Bill's positive persuasion, I finally decided to take the course given by PSI, a decision which has changed my whole outlook on life, and has put everything in its rightful place.

I have since moved to another house and have provided myself and Patches with a comfortable and happy dwelling. A flap door allows her access to the garage where she sleeps at night, or the back yard where she romps during the day. When I greet her first thing after coming home from work, she always looks to me eagerly to play with her bone or to take her for a walk; and I do so because it gives me happiness to do it.

I have taken friends of mine pheasant hunting, and like me, they are amazed at the skill and aggressiveness that Patches displays. She is no longer the antagonizing, attention-getting pest that she once was, and I no longer have the feeling of being "lost" in my life's journey.

My dog and I now have a good relationship. Patches wants to serve me and I give her the opportunities to do so. Whether we walk, play or hunt, she is a true companion, and there is a mutual respect between us. As long as I treat her like a dog, and she looks to me as her master, this relationship will continue to be a good one.

It seems ironic that this dog should have started my whole life changing for the better. But without Patches, or Bill Meisterfeld, who helped steer me in the right direction, I would never be as happy as I am today. To all of those (including Patches) who were responsible for letting me express myself in this story, I give my love.

†Author's note: The PSI-Process is a therapeutic, intensive, in-depth self-analysis which helps you understand your behavior, and which gives tools to bring about change in your life. Its founder is Earnest Pecci, M.D., psychiatrist and Director of PSI Center in Orinda, California.

I believe there is a divine plan and that, when we assume responsibility of being a master, our dog will assume the responsibility of serving us.

Lily

The first day I put a leash on Lily, the Afghan, and took her out to the training ring, she began to scream and flip around like a Mexican jumping bean. I stood still, holding the leash while she had her tantrum. She finally calmed down after she noticed I wasn't responding to her.

I began to walk Lily in the ring. About halfway around she stopped and defecated. I tied her leash to a post, fetched the pick-up can and mop, and cleaned up. We started off again and once more she defecated. Again I tied her to a post and cleaned up after her. This whole process was repeated every twenty feet or so. Finally I put her in her run to finish her toilet so that we could get on with the training.

I checked her an hour later and there were no signs of feces in her run. Thinking she had probably finished, I took her back to the training ring. We had no sooner gotten underway when she defecated once again. It was such a small amount that I wondered why she even bothered. But it was, after all, a strange environment and she may have been unduely nervous. I put Lily away and decided to see what would happen tomorrow.

The next day I had my assistant standing by with the clean-up equipment. It was a wise move for Lily managed to eliminate urine or feces every thirty to forty feet. There was something premeditated about the way in which she doled out the tiny piles and little puddles so regularly. No matter how often I took her outside or left her in the run, she always seemed to save some just for our workouts. It was a favor I could have gladly done without.

I had to take a different course of action to break her habit pattern. Instead of picking up after her as we went around the ring the first time, I just left everything there. The next time we went around, I timed my steps so that when I stopped, she would sit right on her own deposits. I proceeded around the ring stopping at each spot and giving her a sit command if she was reluctant to do so. Both the dog and the training ring needed a thorough cleaning after the session. From that day on, Lily kept all her deposits in reserve.

WHEN I STOPPED AND SHE SAT, SHE LANDED
RIGHT ON HER OWN DEPOSITS.....

Zorba

"Please don't stand up or make any sudden moves when I bring my dog in," Mrs. Taylor said. "He is terribly jumpy and I wouldn't want him to bite you."

"That makes two of us," I said.

She went out to her car to get her dog for the consultation, while I tried to think how best to handle the dog so that I could evaluate him. Mrs. Taylor returned with Zorba, a year-and-a-half-old Doberman cross. He didn't notice me at first, and when he finally did, he bristled from head to tail. A deep growl rumbled in his throat. Mrs. Taylor stroked and talked to him gently until he quieted down. She then brought him closer to me. I knew enough to let the dog get used to me in his own time rather than trying to make friends with him. After sniffing me cautiously, he began to wag his tail. Only then did I venture to pet him. We were friends.

I snapped a leash onto his collar and walked him to his run. Mrs. Taylor had explained to me over the phone how skittish he was, that sometimes he would panic and refuse to go through a strange doorway. So I was prepared for him. I had all the doors leading to the runs opened wide so that I could take him straight through. As a precautionary measure (which I use for all biters) I snapped a twenty-foot-long check cord to his collar before releasing him in his run. I closed and locked the gate and went back to talk more with Mrs. Taylor.

"We originally bought Zorba because we wanted a friendly pet to love," she explained. "I began to socialize him by walking him in the city several times a day. He always seemed shy of strangers but it was never serious until he was about seven months old. That is when he started to growl when people approached us. It got worse as he grew older, until I had to grip the leash with both hands to keep him from attacking people. It doesn't matter if they are men, women, or children, he tries to get them all. Anything sudden, like someone stepping out of an alley, or a car backfiring, will make him jump right out of his skin. My veterinarian recommended either sedation, or putting him to sleep. I didn't want to do either so he gave me your name and said you might be able to help with this problem."

When Mrs. Taylor left, I went into Zorba's run. He was huddled against the far wall in a corner. I repeated his name softly over and over as I inched closer to him. When I was about fifteen feet away, his hackles went up and another ominous growl rumbled in his throat. So much for our "friendship." I backed off a couple feet and he relaxed a little. Picking up the check cord, I turned my back to him and walked out of the run. Zorba followed me as far behind as the cord allowed. I led him to the training ring and began to slowly gather up the slack in the line as we walked around. If he began to resist, I would ease out the line a few inches, only to recover it a few steps later.

I finally got him within four feet of me. I knew from past experience that the last thing I should do in this case would be to try and force him to get close to me. Zorba was genuinely paranoid, and to treat his aggression as a bluff would have been disasterous. I returned him to his run.

Half an hour later I went back to test Zorba's reactions again. This time I'd gotten within thirteen feet before he responded defensively. I picked up the cord and took him to the ring. It took a few minutes less to get him within the four foot range again. It wasn't much, but it was progress nonetheless. I considered my gain positive.

By the time Mrs. Taylor returned for our consultation, I had a pretty clear picture of Zorba's problems. "He shows signs of being abused," I said. Mrs. Taylor looked shocked.

"But we have *never* abused him! We don't believe in that sort of thing."

"I realize that, Mrs. Taylor. I'm not referring to physical abuse however. What I am talking about is emotional abuse. He appears to be humanized."

"What do you mean?"

"I really believe that the kindest thing we can do for our dogs is to be a master to them. A dog feels secure in this type of relationship because he knows if anything unusual comes up, that his master is in charge and can handle it. Now, when we are *not* a master to our dogs, and we treat them as an equal*, they have no one to turn to when something strange happens unexpectedly. Consequently, they feel
*How's & Why's of Psychological Dog Training

166

"WHAT I'M TALKING ABOUT IS EMOTIONAL ABUSE"

that *they* have to deal with everything.

"This is the case with Zorba. His fight-or-flight response, which under normal circumstances is only triggered by immediate danger, is in a constant state of suspense, waiting for something to happen. When something *does* happen, no matter what it is, he has to challenge it until he feels safe and secure with that particular newness. That's what is making Zorba hyper-excitable and paranoid."

Mrs. Taylor listened intently to my explanation. "Yes, I can see your point," she said at last. "I'm afraid my husband is the guilty party. He lets that dog sleep with him—even under the covers. Thank goodness we have separate beds! Charles feeds him 'people food' all the time and always has Zorba on his lap, big as he is. I have never approved of the way he lets the dog do whatever he wants, but I didn't know that that was causing the dog to behave the way he does." She paused. "How long would it take to train him?"

"At least twenty weeks. You realize, of course, that if I train your dog, your husband will have to change his relationship with Zorba."

"Yes, I can see that. I don't know what he would say to having Zorba trained. I think it would be best if I take him home and talk it over with Charles."

I retrieved Zorba (very carefully) and handed him over to Mrs. Taylor, then walked her out to her car.

"I really want this dog trained," she said as she got in the car. "I may have to do some persuading, but you will be hearing from me, Mr. Meisterfeld." She waved as she drove away.

Duchess

The newly washed pick-up pulled along side the front gate and stopped. Ed Madsen popped out of the driver's seat and hurried around the cab with long eager strides to open the passenger door.

Duchess, Ed's Black Labrador, watched intently through the front room window as a strange woman emerged from the pick-up. Smiling coyly the woman took Ed's arm and they strolled toward the house. Duchess had a peculiar sense of foreboding as they neared. It was the same feeling she'd had that morning when things began so differently.

Duchess woke at dawn as usual. She stretched herself out of the overstuffed chair she always slept in, then trotted into her master's bedroom to wake him. This was her self-appointed duty which she always carried out with honor. But this particular morning, Ed was already up. He was—in fact—already dressed and combing his hair in front of the dresser mirror.

"Hello there old girl," he greeted her jovially. "Beat ya to it this morning, didn't I?" Duchess gave him a quizzical look and wagged her tail. He often called her "old girl" although she was not quite two years old.

Ed began whistling loudly as he finished combing his hair. He set the comb down and moved closer to the mirror until his nose was just a few inches away. Still whistling, he examined his face from left and right angles, then finally the patch of thinning hair on the top of his head. He stopped whistling as he carefully arranged more hair to cover it, and then stood back for a final overall appraisal.

Duchess became impatient. They should be outside by now, checking on the cows or gathering eggs from the henhouse for breakfast. And why was he all dressed up instead of in his work clothes?

Next to the dresser was a coat rack on which hung Ed's sport jacket. Ed picked up a lint brush off the dresser and ran it down the jacket a few times. "Well Duch, I have a lot of things to do today," he said putting the jacket on. "I'll leave the back door open for you 'cause I won't be back for awhile."

He started out of the bedroom then stopped as if he'd forgotten something. Turning back he hurriedly picked up all the clothes scattered about the room, threw them in the closet and closed the door. He threw the covers back on the bed and made a clumsy attempt to arrange them neatly. Hurrying into the kitchen he gathered up all the dirty dishes and stashed them under the sink. He surveyed the living room for any more obvious signs of bachelorhood. Apparently satisfied, he started to leave. Duchess, who had been following him around the house, bounded for the door. Ed laughed as he took a pair of mirrored sunglasses out of the front pocket of his jacket and put them on.

"Sorry old girl. You're not coming with me this time. You take care of the place 'till I get back." he patted her on the head then closed the door on her puzzled face.

"Well, this must be Duchess." the woman said as she and Ed entered the house. The woman kneeled down and offered her hand to the dog. Duchess sniffed at it suspiciously then turned away to greet Ed.

"Now that's no way to treat company." Ed chided. Turning to the woman, "Don't mind her Darla, she's not used to company. We lead a pretty solitary life out here."

Ed steered his lady friend into the living room and Duchess was virtually forgotten as they chatted and laughed together.

A seed of resentment began to sprout inside of Duchess. She didn't like this woman who had such a strange effect on Ed. All Duchess wanted was for things to be the way they were. She picked an unobtrusive spot in the livingroom that afforded a good view of Ed and the lady, and plopped down to watch them—and sulk. She knew she wouldn't feel right again until the stranger left. For good.

The evening wore on. Ed mixed drinks and set out bowls of cheese curls and mixed nuts. The talk and laughter rose and flowed as the atmosphere became relaxed. Still there was no indication that the woman was going to leave.

Duchess, up to this point, had been very patient. Now she was beginning to fret. Perhaps a few subtle hints would help move things along. She got up and went to the front door and waited for them to notice. But the couple (who now were sitting very close together on

A STRANGE WOMAN EMERGED FROM THE PICK-UP...

the couch) were oblivious to everything but each other.

Duchess realized she would have to be a little more explicit. She walked up and rested her muzzle on Ed's knee and looked up at him with a baleful expression. Without looking at her, or breaking the conversation, Ed gently pushed the dog's head away. Duchess whined and nuzzled Ed, forcing him to notice her. "Stop it Duchess! Go lie down," he said annoyed. Duchess stood defiantly.

"Excuse me, Darla," he said apologetically. "She's acting pretty queer. I'm going to put her out back." He took hold of the dog's collar and led her out to the back yard. "If you can't behave you'll just have to stay out here tonight," he said and closed the back door behind him.

At no time could Duchess remember being treated this way. She had never known the hurt and humiliation of being banished outside. She felt the anger inside of her build up. She walked in circles trying to alleviate her distress but it welled up and up until it forced itself out of her throat in the form of a long siren-like howl. Again she howled, letting her anguish vent itself. Now she was getting into the stream of it as another lament escaped, building, rising to a most astonishing crescendo. So involved was she in pouring out her sorrows to the world, that she didn't notice the back door open. Or the hand that reached down to pick up a work boot. Or when it shot out toward her. She only felt it land smartly on the end of her crescendo. Duchess let out a surprised yelp.

"Now shut up!" Ed hollered and slammed the door. She did. Ed returned to Darla, and Duchess was dismissed from his mind for the rest of the night.

The next morning the back door opened up and Ed appeared. "C'mon Duch," he called clapping his hands twice. Duchess remained curled up next to the hen house where she had spent the night. She would not enter the house while that woman was still there.

"Suit yourself," Ed said as he went back inside, leaving the door open for her. Duchess waited. She heard a door shut on the pick-up, then another. The engine came to life and the truck drove away.

Duchess felt a strong urge to avenge her wounded pride. She entered the house and went straight to Ed's bedroom, all the while sensing that she didn't have too much time before his return. She brightened when she saw Ed's sport jacket still hanging on the coat rack. And there, in the pocket, were his sunglasses. Perfect!

She jumped up on the rumpled bed then onto the nightstand where she balanced precariously on it's small surface. Then, cat-like, she leaped up onto the dresser which was next to the nightstand. Duchess slunk toward the sport jacket with determination. She was

DUCHESS FELT A STRONG URGE TO AVENGE
HER WOUNDED PRIDE...

momentarily sidetracked, however, when the comb and lint brush that lay in her path caught her attention. Within minutes she had chewed the comb and lint brush beyond recognition. Then she turned her attention back to her original objective—Ed's sunglasses.

She neared the jacket, the pocket was almost level with her head. She crouched down at the edge of the dresser and straining her neck forward, grasped the protruding part of the glasses firmly in her front teeth and pulled back. Instantly the jacket loomed above which startled her into letting go. The coat rack and jacket swung back, teetered momentarily, then came to rest again. Duchess tried again. Straining, she took hold and jerked the glasses out of the pocket. The coat rack careened forward, then back on two legs where it remained suspended for several seconds before returning with a thud in its upright position. Duchess jumped down on the floor, then back on to the bed to complete the job she'd set out to do.

It wasn't long before Duchess heard the familiar sound of the pick-up outside. She ran to the window in time to see Ed walking and whistling to the front door.

"Hey Duch old girl! How ya doin', huh?" he said happily rough-housing her when she met him at the door. Duchess responded jubiliantly. *This* was the Ed she knew.

"I'll go change, then we'll go check those cows, how's that?" Duchess didn't follow him as he went into the bedroom whistling. She listened to the tuneless melody and the rumaging sounds coming out of the room. Then there was silence.

"Duchess!" The dog crept slowly into the bedroom to face an angry Ed. "Do you see this?" he said pointing to a gnarled mass of plastic projections that was once his comb. "And this?" pointing to the lint brush with the bristles scattered around it like pine needles. "And *this!*" he said more forcefully, jabbing a finger at the tangled remains of his sunglasses lying smack in the middle of his bed.

Duchess lowered her head and shifted her eyes around the room to avoid looking at her master. Ed plunked down on the edge of the bed. "Why?" he said to no one in particular. Duchess inched forward, her belly almost touching the ground, and rested her head on Ed's knee apologetically. Ed was searching for an explanation for her odd behavior when a thought came to him. He looked down at Duchess as if seeing her for the first time.

"It was Darla, wasn't it?" he said. "You're jealous aren't you Duch?" Duchess' tail thumped twice. Ed shook his head. "I never would have thought it. A jealous dog. What am I going to do with you Duch?" She rolled her eyes up to look at him. Ed let out a long slow sigh. "Well, c'mon girl, let's go check those cows."

One, Two, Three, You're Out!

When I was working as a hunting guide at the Nimrod Club in Elyria, Ohio, I was the guide for a party of five men who had flown in from Michigan. The host was a promotional manager for a large national cereal company. He explained that he was an avid bird hunter, but his clients had never hunted before. Since he wanted them to enjoy themselves, he asked me to make sure they all got some shooting in. I was understandably reluctant to do this. One inexperienced gunner I could handle, but *four* of them was downright dangerous. I agreed to take them, however, on the basis that I would be in full charge—not only of the hunt, but who was to shoot as well.

The men lined up in a single row and I took my place in the center so that I could watch everyone and handle Baroness at the same time. We started walking and Baroness began to sweep the area in front of us like a windshield wiper, from left to right. She quickly developed a pattern, running about twenty-five feet beyond the man at one end, then sweeping parallel to our line and twenty-five feet beyond the man at the other end. This gave full and thorough coverage of the area in front of us.

Baroness found several pheasants and some of the men were able to bag them. But one fellow on the right end had managed to miss three birds in a row. After the third miss, Baroness changed her hunting pattern. She covered the ground for the fourth man on the right, then she would turn and sweep left; this completely cut out number five who kept missing. That meant that he would not get anymore shooting in, which would make his host unhappy. As long as I commanded her, Baroness would cover his territory. But if I stopped whistling, she would refuse to hunt for him. Finally I had to switch number five to number three's spot. Baroness then gave full wiping range to everyone.

Number five never asked me why I moved him, and I never attempted to explain. But I had a feeling he knew anyway.

MISSED THREE PHEASANTS IN A ROW.....

The Vacation

Miss Heath was an attractive woman. No doubt about it. She swung into my office with long slow strides, sat down opposite me and crossed her legs. She appeared to me to be oddly dressed for the occasion; short skirt, low blouse, elbow length gloves, and knee-high boots.

"I just *love* Wally more than anything else in the world!" she gushed.

"Wally?" I repeated weakly. Who in the world is Wally? I thought.

"Yes, my dog, Wallabee. I call him Wally for short. He's such a dear."

"Oh, yes, Wallabee, your dog. Of course," I babbled. She certainly was stunning.

"As much as I love him though, he has a few . . . quirks, you might call them. That's why I came to you. I was hoping you could help me."

"What kind of quirks?"

"Well, I'd like to have a little more control over him in certain situations. He's such a friendly love that he jumps all over people. Sometimes he even pulls me down the street if he sees dogs or people he wants to play with, sweet thing." She chuckled softly and shook her head. "I want to be able to play with him, but maybe you can teach him to play a little more . . . gently?" She smiled and fixed her lovely dark eyes on mine. More gently? Those last words seemed to hang in the air. Without preliminaries she daintily plucked the fingers of her right hand and removed her glove. Slowly, she bent forward and unzipped one boot, then the other.

I stared dumbly. I have a rule never to mix business with pleasure, but Miss Heath seemed to have other ideas. She removed each boot.

"This is how we play," she said, extending her hand out to me with a big smile. I felt my face flush crimson. Ohio was never like *this*!

I was so involved in confusion and conflict that I didn't notice her other hand pointing to something.

"This is how Wally and I play," she said a little louder. I stared at her arm as she pointed to all the scars and scratches she had acquired from "playing" with Wally. Her legs, she also pointed out, were scarred in the same way.

I finally realized that she was not making advances toward me at all. I cleared my throat and gathered my professional air about me once again. "How, ah, long has he been doing this?"

"Ever since he was a pup. It's his nails you see. And his teeth. As I mentioned, he does jump quite a bit. And he likes to grab my arm or leg when he wants to play. But if he gets too excited he nips too hard sometimes and makes me bleed. I usually wear old gloves and boots around the house because of him; but I can't be prepared *all* the time, can I? I mean, I can't wear them to bed or in the tub."

"You mean you've allowed this to go on for over *four* years?" I asked incredulously. "Why didn't you stop it the first time he hurt you?"

"Well, he doesn't *mean* to hurt me," she said defensively. "He's only expressing his love for me in the only way he knows. How can I punish him for that?"

What a definition of love, I thought. He loves her like he loves a good bone. "Miss Heath," I began in my most convincing tone, "love is supposed to be pleasurable, not painful. Believe me when I say that Wally bites you not from love, but from lack of respect. He has established himself as your superior, and you as his chew toy."

"I just don't want to hurt him" she retorted.

I felt a seed of anger within me. Her defense of Wally's abuse had touched a sensitive nerve of mine. I have had other clients that felt the same way. To them, discipline means physical punishment, which will therefore discourage their pet's affection. This is an erroneous concept. Discipline is merely outlining and maintaining a behavioral structure. I explained at length how the average dog's mind functions, and what Wally's actions meant in reality. I drew pictures on a blackboard that emhasized proper master/dog relationships and so on.

Miss Heath looked thoughtful. "I think I understand what you're saying," she said at last. "Perhaps it would be best for Wally to get some education." She paused again. "Yes, I think that *would* be best."

"Fine. I have a contract here for you to fill out and sign, then Wally will be in."

"Oh, by the way," she spoke as she was almost finished writing. "How often can I visit him?"

"Not at all until he's finished with his schoolwork."

Miss Heath stopped in the middle of signing her name and looked at me aghast. "Not even once a week? B-but he'll miss me. I'll miss him. . ."

"Wally will be occupied with his training," I said, trying to sound reassuring. "He'll have plenty to do. Visits from you before he's ready will give me too many setbacks in the training."

"I suppose," she said edgily, then finished signing her name. We set up a tentative date ten weeks away for her first training session with Wally.

"One thing I should mention, Miss Heath. There is a possibility of my taking a week's vacation in the first part of February. If I do I'll put all the dogs here, including Wally, on free boarding for that week."

The woman's face clouded. "Who's going to take care of him?"

"A friend of mine is going to be staying here while I'm gone. Her name is Mrs. Dury."

"But does she know anything about dogs?"

"Inside and out. She's been a highly reputable dog breeder for fifteen years."

"I see," she said skeptically. "As long as Wally's all right." With that she thanked me and departed. Strange sort of woman, I thought.

She called almost everyday those first weeks to find out how "My sweet Wallabee" was doing. With my constant reassurance that Wally had taken well to training, her calls diminished. Wally was basically a good dog in spite of his bad habits. He tried to nip me once, but a firm correction was all it took to convince him not to do it again. All he needed (and he seemed to sense this) was a master who required respect. Almost automatically, Wally respected me for establishing his behavioral boundaries. He was a born worker, only up until now, he was never required to do so. Within a month he had made rapid progress.

Then my opportunity came for a vacation in the Hawaiian Islands. I made arrangements with Mrs. Dury to live in so there would be someone on the premises twenty-four hours a day. Training for the dogs would be suspended until I returned.

I called Mrs. Heath (as I did all my other clients) and explained the situation to her. I gave her my departure and return dates and assured her again that Wallabee was fine, and that there was nothing to worry about. She seemed satisfied.

I took off from San Francisco International Airport on a Friday, watching the people and buildings get smaller and smaller as we

WALLY REALLY WAS A GOOD DOG IN SPITE OF
HIS BAD HABITS.....

ascended. The plane banked into a wide turn, then headed out to sea. This was my first real vacation in years and it was an exquisite feeling. About five hours later we landed in the tropical paradise known as Hawaii; land of *mahimahi*, hula dancers and sunburns. I stepped out of the plane and took a deep breath of the warm, humid air— *Hawaiian air!* I descended the steps two at a time, eager to begin my much needed respite.

I spent every day snorkling in the warm crystal clear water, collecting souveniers of finger, lace and brain coral. I spent endless hours among the colorful fish that abound in the reefs; fish of every hue and shape imaginable. Such a different world from the one I had left. Thoughts of neurotic dogs were far away as the tropical sun and water washed over me.

As always, when one is immersed in his surroundings, the time whips by. Nine days later I reluctantly boarded the aircraft that would take me home. As an extra treat to myself, I flew first class. Leaning back, I listened to the twanging island music coming through my headsets. I wanted to hang on to Hawaii for as long as I could.

I got off the plane in San Francisco, looking all the part of a *Malahini* returning to the mainland. It was not hard to guess where I'd been. I was brown as a coconut, wearing my flowered Hawaiian shirt, leather sandals, and carrying a bag of Little Boy Flowers (Anthuriums). I even wore what I thought to be an excellent imitation of a beach-boy grin. Yep, I felt good enough for another 100,000 miles. I found a pay phone and, with the crashing surf still echoing in my ears, I dialed home. Mrs. Dury answered.

"Aloha, aloha!" I boomed. "How's. . ."

"Oh gods, where were you?" she interrupted. "We've been trying to find you all week." I hadn't told anyone where I was staying, nor did I bother to call. I hadn't foreseen any problems.

"It's that Heath woman. She called a couple days after you left and wanted to see Wally. I told her I couldn't let her visit while you were gone. I asked her if you'd contacted her about your trip and she said 'yes,' but she still wanted to see her dog. I told her I was sorry but I had my instructions. Monday she called *four* times trying to wheedle her way in. I just wouldn't do it. I told her flat out to call when you got back. Then she got mad and said, 'I don't believe you have Wally in the kennel. Did he die? Or did that trainer sell him?' "

I could hardly believe this was happening. I felt the anger rising inside me. "What *is* the matter with that woman?" I said heatedly.

"That's just the beginning," Mrs. Dury said. "I tried to tell her Wally was fine and that you'd be back within a week, but she hung up on me. That afternoon the Sonoma County Deputy Sheriff stopped over, at her lawyer's request, he said. I showed him the dog and he wrote out a detailed description. We both thought that would be proof enough that her dog was alive and well. Wednesday morning he came back and told me that Miss Heath said it sounded like her dog but that it didn't prove it was. She still insisted on seeing him herself to make sure. The deputy advised me to let her or she might get a court order. It was getting so ridiculous! I called her and she came right away. I let her see him from a distance, but I told her not to let him know she was there. I still didn't want her to goof up the training you have in him. Well, several dogs barked as we came around the far building to peek at him, and Wally was one of them. That seemed to satisfy her and she left."

"Good," I said, feeling better. "You handled that wonderfully. I'm sorry it had to happen while I was gone."

"That's *still* not all," she sighed. "She called again late Wednesday evening and wanted to take him home, then return him the following Monday when you were due back. I told her I couldn't break the contract she had signed, and that I did not have the authority to release her dog. And since I couldn't make contact with you, she would *just have to wait until next Monday*. Thursday morning her attorney called and advised me to turn Wally over to Miss Heath, or he would have to get a court order. Well, I tell you I had just *had it* with that woman! I called her up and told her to come get her dog, so she did."

As I listened to the whole thing, I felt the magic of the islands slipping away from me. My vacation was over. "Oh well," I mumbled. "At least it's over with."

"Not quite."

I straightened up. "Whatd'ya mean, 'not quite'? What more can happen?" I snapped, dropping my bag of Boy Flowers.

"She's sueing you for five thousand dollars. Something to do with mental cruelty, emotional injuries or something like that. The deputy stopped by with the summons for you. . ."

"I don't want to hear anymore," I groaned. "Tell me the rest when I get there." I hung up the phone, bought a cup of coffee and headed back to the lounge area. I wove through crowds returning from who knows where, and arrived at a seating area which was practically empty. I sat down and watched the planes taking off, picturing myself getting on one of them and going back to the warm tranquility of the islands. Closing my eyes, I was once again a part of the crystal ocean, swaying with the gentle currents. I opened my eyes. It just wasn't fair.

Monday I called a friend of mine whom I knew had been in a similar situation. I thought maybe he could give me some helpful advice.

"Countersuit!" he declared, after I'd told him the story.

"Countersuit?"

"Darn right! for defamation of character. Either that or hire an attorney to protect yourself. She'll take you to the cleaners if you don't. I'd bet on it."

"Thanks, John. I'll think about it." I hung up the phone, dejected. All of a sudden it looked like I was going to have to shell out a good deal of money for this nightmare. It was getting more unbelievable every minute. If there were only someone I could count on for some sound legal advice. . .

Rollie! *That's* the person! Rolland Webb, the honorable judge of Petaluma. My friend! I had met Rollie years ago. He was always an amiable guy, and he had the most astounding repertoire of jokes of anyone else I knew. In those days we used to play "Beat the Hand," which is a cupped dice game. I won a side bet with him once which he never forgot. He always kidded that he would get even if I ever came to his court. But I never took him seriously, and now I was counting on him.

Rollie met me with a solemn face and motioned me to have a seat in his chamber. I didn't know quite what to make of his coolness toward me but I began my story anyway. As I recounted in detail the sequence of events, I noticed that he was starting to chuckle. The more fervent I became the harder he laughed. I did *not* think it was funny and was truly annoyed by his behavior. By the time I'd finished my story I was full of resentment toward him.

"So *this* is your way of paying me back!" I shot out. "I came to you with a serious problem and you don't even care. I never thought that stupid bet was so important that you'd laugh at a friend in need." I got up to leave. Enough was enough.

"Sit down, Bill," he said soberly. The look on his smiling face was kind. "Do you want to make money off this confused woman? If you do then I would say countersuit." Before I could answer he went on. "Knowing you, I don't think that's what you want. So, for six dollars, and without an attorney, you can file a denial. This I would advise you to do. And don't worry, once she settles down with her dog, her attorney will more than likely advise her to drop the suit because there was a contract binding her to ten weeks. There are no grounds for her claim."

"Oh, man, is *that* a relief! Thanks, Rollie. Sorry I got so heated up, but this thing has had me on edge, if you know what I mean."

He waved my apology aside. "Forget it, Bill. But I'll tell you what; why don't you clip my poodle's nails when you can?" Then his eyes lit up as if he had just remembered something. "Hey, did you hear the one about. . ."

I left Rollie's chamber feeling much better than when I'd gone in. I went to my car laughing at his outrageous jokes, and for the relief I felt.

I took his advice and filed a denial and two days later, Miss Heath dropped the lawsuit. My nightmare was over, but what a price to pay for nine days away. I still wonder if it was worth it.

Ming

Ming felt the sharp pain welling inside her again. She strained hard and felt the pain give way to something else. She instinctively curled around, broke and ate the sac off of her new-born pup. Then, from head to tail, she massaged it with her tongue. It wasn't long before another pup emerged, and she repeated the process. There were only two, both sons, but Ming was as happy as any mother could be. She looked up at the ring of smiling faces that had been silently watching. Ray, Linda and their three children had gathered around Ming's nest to watch the miracle of birth. Linda had a special reason for wanting to be there; she wanted to be available in case the little Maltese needed help with her delivery. This was, after all, Ming's first litter and she was already three years old. But Linda's concern turned out to be unfounded.

Mothering was a serious business to Ming. She stayed right with her pups and only left her nest to relieve herself outside. She was always there whenever her pups were hungry and she made certain that they were relieved regularly. It was her instinct to stimulate and ingest their eliminations by massaging their genital areas with her tongue. This kept her nest clean and tidy.

Ray and Linda were especially pleased with the pups. They had planned to keep them and, from all appearances, they'd made the right choice. The children were also delighted. They watched Ming and her pups for hours on end. They often reached in to tickle a tiny head or run a finger down their soft backs. Once in a while they would lift one out and examine it at close range. Ming allowed this— grudgingly. But after a couple of minutes she would noisily demand that her pup be returned. Once back in the nest, she would nose it over thoroughly until she was satisfied that all its parts were still there. The children named the first-born, "Won," and the second one, "Tu."

It didn't seem long before Won and Tu's eyes began to open up to a blurry new world. As the days passed and their vision became more clear, their individualities began to emerge. Won appeared to be the boldest of the two. He was the first to discover the use of his legs and he spent much time exercising them. Tu was more the introvert, usually following his brother's lead, or staying close to Ming.

Ming enjoyed a luxury that most brood bitches do not always get; that is, her pups were never taken from her. Her capacity to "mother" was seemingly boundless. But, as we all know, puppies do not remain puppies forever. The time came when even the complacent nature of Tu was stirred with the need to relieve himself outside the nest. But whenever Ming saw a pup toddling away, she would grasp it by the neck and haul it back. Consequently, she continued to ingest her puppies eliminations in order to keep the nest clean.

In an attempt to help get Ming past her reluctance to give the pups more freedom, Linda removed the box in which they had been living, and replaced it with some blanket bedding. The abruptness of the change made Tu fearful, and he hung close to his mother's side. On the other hand, Won seemed delighted. He quickly scouted the boundaries of the blanket under the ever watchful eye of Ming. Won felt a surge of excitement that made him almost giddy. He trotted over to Tu and batted the top of his head with his paw. Tu, who did not share his brother's enthusiasm, whimpered and cringed. Undaunted, Won boldly trotted off the blanket to explore what seemed to be the endless expanse of the living room. He had barely gotten underway when he felt the familiar grip on his neck, and protesting loudly, was dragged back to the blanket by Ming. It looked like his struggle for independence was going to be a long one.

By the time the puppies were several months old, it was nearly impossible for Ming to keep them all together, and she was beginning to feel the strain of the effort. Since her whelping box had been taken away, Ming considered the entire house to be her nest. And although Linda had been in the process of house-breaking the pups, Ming, who had not broken her maternal habit of ingesting their feces, still insisted on cleaning up their mistakes. She was fighting a losing battle to hang onto her motherhood and it was beginning to take its toll. She had lost weight as well as her temper. Trying to keep track of her pups was an exhausting affair. Rarely did she have time to sleep or even rest. Even shy little Tu was known to go off on his own at times, making her job twice as hard. But Ming stubbornly refused to let got of her maternal role.

Ming's breaking point came one day when she was catching a few minutes of exhausted sleep. She had just gathered up Won and Tu and they were fast asleep on the couch next to her. Suddenly Won awoke to a noise. Without hesitation, he jumped off the couch to investigate. There was someone or something outside the back door and as Won neared the door, he began to bark. Ming awoke. Alarmed that Won was gone, she sped away to find him. Amidst all the commotion Tu also awoke, and finding himself abandoned, began to wail pitfully. Ming ran back in an instant to comfort Tu. Meanwhile, Won lost interest in the noise he'd heard and wandered upstairs. In the bathroom he found an earwig and tried to hold the intruder at bay. Ming heard Won's bark echoing off the bathroom walls and was completely baffled as to where it was coming from. She bounded in and out of all the rooms on the first floor looking for Won. Finally she made it upstairs and found him. By this time, Tu had wandered off looking for someone, *anyone* to comfort him. Finding no one, he plunked himself down and let out a heart-wrenching cry. Ming streaked down the stairs with Won at her heels. It happened that one of the children had also heard Tu, and had taken him into the den. Ming arrived, panting and worried. Finding Tu was not where she'd left him sent her into another panicked search. Won, clearly bored, wandered off once more leaving his mother to her frenzied state.

It was all just too much for Ming. Linda happened by and found the little dog huddled in a corner looking hopeless. "What's wrong, Ming?" Linda spoke soothingly and reached down to pick her up. The last thing Ming wanted was someone hovering around her. She watched Linda's hands get closer and just before they reached her, Ming snapped at them. The woman recoiled in shock. It was the first time Ming had ever snapped at anyone. Shaken, Linda left her there and ran to find Ray.

The next thing Ming knew she was perched atop a table, and safely muzzled, was being poked and probed quite thoroughly. How she got there was a vague blur. Linda waited anxiously as the veterinarian completed his examination of Ming.

"I can't find anything physically wrong with her," he said at last. "She appears to be highly nervous though. I'll give you some mild tranquilizers to give her; they'll probably help, but they're not the best solution."

"We have to do *something*," Linda said, worriedly. "She's just wasting away, poor thing. She's become so morose and crotchety that we are all afraid to get near her."

The doctor thought for a moment. "Here's something you might want to look into," he said. He opened a drawer, pulled out a card and handed it to her.

"Hello, Ray?" Linda said into the phone. "I'm calling from Meisterfeld Kennels. I came here straight from the doctor's office." Ming sat forlornly on the office carpet, listening to the conversation.

"I told Mr. Meisterfeld, the trainer, about our situation and he checked Ming out. He figured out what the trouble is alright. It's the pups. She couldn't wean herself from them—psychologically speaking, that is. That is what's causing her problem." Linda paused, listening. "Well, Mr. Meisterfeld said that what she needs most is rest and recuperation. It might also be good to leave her for some training. What do you think?" Linda smiled into the phone. "Great! See you later." She hung up the phone and gave the okay signal to the man sitting at the desk.

Ming was led into a large enclosure. She sensed the presence of other dogs nearby, but she didn't seem to care. They didn't belong to her and she wouldn't have to clean up after them. She ambled outside, sought a place to lie down in the sun, and fell asleep to the peaceful sound of birds chirping.

A PLACE TO LIE DOWN IN THE SUN.....

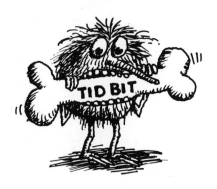

Love does not conquer a problem dog.

Ambush!

Although Von, the German Shepherd, outweighed Pierpont, the Minature Poodle, by about seventy-five pounds, they were nevertheless best of friends. This unlikely duo were partners in a continual campaign to harass their next door neighbor, a Standard Poodle named Jacques.

At least once a week, Pierpont would boldly cross over into Jacques' home territory to pester him. Meanwhile, Von would station himself around the back corner of the house—and wait.

When Jacques could no longer endure Pierpont's high-pitched insults, the big Poodle would angrily chase him out of his yard. This was what Pierpont was hoping for. The little Poodle ran out of the neighboring yard and onto his own driveway, with Jacques in close pursuit. As they turned the back corner of the house, Von would leap out and land on top of Jacques. After a brief scuffle, Jacques, more startled than hurt, would run home yelping.

It was a clever scheme, and skillfully executed; and although it never varied, poor Jacques never did catch on.

VON WOULD LEAP OUT AND LAND ON TOP OF JACQUES...

Blindman's Bluff

One of the tests a dog must go through in a retrieving trial is called a "blind retrieve." This is where the dog is placed behind a four-foot-high free standing "blind," which is comparable to a folding panel screen. The handler watches as the bird is placed in the cover across the duck pond. He is then required to send his dog across the water and, using directional signals, guide the dog to the planted bird.

When I was first training Baroness, my German Shorthair Pointer, for these trails, I parked my station wagon parallel to the riverbank and used it as an improvised blind. I gave Baroness a *sit-stay* command about a foot away from the driver's door, facing it. Then I hopped in my boat, rowed across the river, placed a bumper in the high weeds and rowed back. I took Baroness down to the river and gave her an "across" command. Once on the other side, I directed her to the bumper location. After she had retrieved the bumper and delivered it to me, I would repeat the process, hiding the bumper in a different spot each time.

Baroness loved nothing more than to hunt, and within a few days she was doing exceptionally well on the blind retrieves. I marveled at how she seemed to anticipate my directions. It appeared she didn't even need any handling. She was almost . . . well, *too* good. I began to notice that she always swam straight for the bumper, no matter where I hid it. It was not possible that she could have tracked me through the water.

I decided to test her by rowing down wind and concealing the bumper under some river debris along the opposite bank. I rowed back and walked up the bank to get Baroness. She was sitting in her usual place facing the car. I took her down to the water and sent her off. Without any handling on my part, Baroness swam straight to where I'd hidden the bumper, dug it out of the debris and brought it back to me.

I was trying to figure out how she knew exactly where to go on a blind retrieve when my neighbor hailed me from next door.

"Did you see Baroness just now, Joe?" I asked. "She found that bumper all by herself! She's either reading my mind or she has x-ray eyes."

Joe laughed. "Neither one," he said. "I saw the whole thing and I think that dog o' yours is smarter'n you are. When you got in the boat, she dropped down on all fours and watched from underneath the car. When you got in the boat to come back, she sat up again."

I guess she was smarter than me, at that!

I GUESS SHE WAS SMARTER THAN ME, AT THAT !...

Charlie
by Gina George

My story is filled with drama, incident, love and tragedy. Only in as far as the sensational aspects make my message more vivid and memorable do I seek to relate them. This message is directed to the countless women who have doting, passionate relationships with their animals (dogs specifically) and while these bonds can be fully rewarding and deeply joyful and may never come to grief, there will be those that, because of the very nature of these bonds, will move inexorably towards disaster. Mine is such a story.

Charlie (born Diskin on Dec. 14, 1972) is a beautiful black and golden-tan German Shepherd of championship stock who, had he not had his problems, would surely have won some dog show prizes. I wanted a male, I think, for no other reason (at the time) than that I had had a female before and wanted a change. Right at this point I should have stopped and searched my soul. Why did I really want a male? In view of how I thought and felt later it's clear that I was charmed by the idea of having a male be my protector. Not that Lisa (my other dog) hadn't protected me, but we *know* that males are supposed to be the true protectors. I was probably responding to some inner prompting which urged me as a female to find my male defender. "Me Tarzan, you Jane!" Why a human male couldn't take on this role (though I was attached to one) is unclear to me. Could it be that tradition is losing its hold in view of the new push towards equality between males and females? Anyway I picked a male, and not only faulted on this, but I picked him because he was quiet and withdrawn instead of friendly and scrappy like the other pups. I thought his behavior was sweet, and it inspired the mother instinct in me to protect and shield "my baby" from the scary world around him. Little did I realize that this protector and baby, aided and abetted by me, was going to play out his role to the hilt!

It's not as though I didn't have fair warning. Two days after I brought him home, he responded aggressively and fearfully when handled by the veterinarian. The doctor promptly told me that, if I weren't too attached to him already, I should give him up, since Diskin was "neurotic and paranoid" and when he grew up he would cost me a great deal of money to train. But giving him up was out of the question—I was already in love. I was determined though, to bring up my dog so that by the time he became a teenager, I wouldn't have a brat, or a criminal-minded beast, but a loveable, well-adjusted dog.

So I began my efforts dilligently. I would be very disciplined at first, then I'd slowly, slowly peter out. This weakness really was the crux of all my problems, and something which I believe I share with many, many others. The fact is, I wouldn't, couldn't follow through with my disciplinary measures. I simply lacked discipline myself, and if we lack it, then no matter how we are motivated by love or whatever to achieve our goals, we will not succeed. It seems almost trite to be restating something that has become almost axiomatic, and yet it appears we need to be reminded again and again. Sometimes I suspect that the only way we acquire discipline is through the severe consequences of our actions. But I'm jumping ahead a little here—as I say, I set about trying to cure my pet of his fear of people. For example, we'd go and spend time at the bus-stop where there were lots of people bustling about. Not much success though. He would always be hiding behind me or burying his head under my arm so that he wouldn't see or be seen.

Then came time for First Grade. We went off to school together once a week to learn how to do all those good things dogs are supposed to do. Sure enough, Diskin excelled in class—he did everything perfectly. But when we got out, guess who was pulling whom around! And he was getting pretty strong too. At first we practiced everyday, then one or two days would go by before I'd try again. In the meantime I pampered, coddled and loved him without restraint.

One day when he was a little over one year old, Diskin's brattiness took a really serious turn. We were walking when he espied a little boy further up the hill. Promptly Diskin took off after him. It was luck and quick reaction on the child's part that saved him from getting more than a nick on his arm. I reprimanded Diskin severely. He was crestfallen and shamefaced; he hadn't really meant to do it but "you know how it is mum, I just lost control. . ." Well, we took off for Mexico anyway as planned that same day. Bill Meisterfeld (who was later to take him in hand) pointed out that this was quite a mistake. It was as if I were rewarding him by immediately taking off in the car (which he loved) on a long trip.

Six months later, the inevitable happened again, only this time he bit a man in the seat of his pants, who was trying to save his cats from being attacked by Diskin and some other dogs. It was now quite apparent that I had a real problem on my hands. I could never trust that he wouldn't simply dash out after someone, and if he were on leash, it was a question of my strength against his. He'd become in short, quite unmanageable—a spoiled "child," but never, thank God, a truly vicious dog. His underlying problem was that he feared people and this manifested itself in cowardly attacks on creatures who were either weaker or at some disadvantage. The trouble was that in time he could very well become more plucky and do some real harm.

Diskin was one and a half years old when Bill Meisterfeld came into his life. During the five months that Bill had him, he made Diskin work like a dog. Everyday he learned and relearned what his limits were. His world was *defined* for him, his position in it, and how this related to his master. At the end of those five months, Charlie Brown (we'd changed his name so that it would take him down a peg or two in my eyes) came home transformed. I'd also changed supposedly. I'd gone to PSI to reeducate myself so that I wouldn't pamper, coddle and smother my dog with love. I would be the master. Charlie wasn't going to run all over *me* etc. etc.

So it was that we happily started out on this new path. Everything went fine for a while. Charlie slept outside in a kennel instead of on my bed, I refrained from kissing and otherwise expressing my love, and we did our lessons everyday. Then the dam burst. It was torturous for me not to demonstrate my love. I could not give this love in measured doses. The nature of my feeling demanded expression—extravagant expression. It was impossible—those limpid, beguiling, brown eyes would melt my heart, and he knew it. He had an arsenal of charms to bombard my defenses, and he used them mercilessly. He was always a great cajoler, and I must confess, I loved being manipulated in this way... But when this emotional dam burst, lo and behold, Charlie was able to handle it, give it back in full measure and still be an obedient dog. Bill had done an excellent job, and Charlie had too. He could have reverted, but didn't. Somewhere in his psyche, Charlie had decided that he wouldn't let his mistress garble up his life. At least as far as his relationship with people went. During his time with Bill, he learned to let go of his fears, and he came around to learning *respect* instead. And so it is that I'll never have to worry about Charlie biting again. Thus ends this chapter of Charlie's life—happily. But my lack of consistency as far as discipline was concerned, was still to rebound on me with a cruel and final lesson.

It happened in Los Angeles one and a half years ago. Charlie was four. I had kept up his training as far as heeling and sitting went. I was afraid he would be struck by a car, so (during the day) these commands were always in force when we'd come to curbside. Night was another matter. On beautiful balmy evenings, I'd take walks and would become lax with my commands. It came about that he would walk and run quite freely across those deserted side streets without a word from me. I wasn't afraid; after all, there were no cars around.

On that fateful night, Nov. 13, 1976, Charlie had been on his leash, and I had just turned him loose to do what he had to do before we turned in, when he saw a dog about a half block away across the main street. Boom, he was gone like a shot, and as he crossed the street he was struck. He could have died right then and it would have been a fearsome lesson to me, but I wasn't going to be let off so easily. Both his back legs were injured; one leg was broken, the other dislocated.

Three weeks later, Charlie's life was still hanging by a thread. Infection raged, and I was beside myself with the horror of it all. Charlie's only hope was the veterinarian school at Davis, California. Four months went by. Four months of hope, despair, renewed hope and finally, in April 1977, he was released a three-legged dog, suffering from a bad case of muscle atrophy in the third leg. The bill was upwards of $4,000, and I had experienced much, much anguish— not to mention Charlie's pain. It has been a full year since his release. I will never have to worry about his dashing out into the street—he simply cannot move very fast anymore. . .

We women who own dogs, especially if we're single, can fall into a dangerous trap when we love our animals madly. Because they're "only dogs" we often give full reign to our mothering instinct, our need to feel protected, our emotional love needs. We wouldn't treat a child this way, after all he might grow up emotionally disturbed. Then why do we so conveniently forget, and treat our animals this way? I know *I* can't answer this—I'm one of the culprits. Even so, there is something deeply satisfying for me in being able to give full vent to my love feelings with my pet. The relationship becomes deep, complete and joyful. The fact is, there are relationships that no matter how deep, how emotionally charged, the animal remains sane, healthy and obedient. My old dog Lisa is a perfect testimonial to this. Even Charlie has shown amazing adaptability and recuperative powers. In so many

ways they are like us!

Theoretically we're all capable of so much more, but in practice, again and again we fall short of the ideal. So my message is, in essence, be aware of your desires and limitations and choose your future pet based on this knowledge of yourself. This means, referring back to me as an example, *no more males!* I recognize this subterranean desire was the root of much of my trouble. But as far as my inability to be a consistant and thorough trainer, I think I've actually undergone some profound changes. In the future, consistent discipline will be a must. It's funny but in view of what has happened to me, maintaining discipline won't be something I *have* to do, but something I *automatically* do, like breathing and eating—to live.

It is tragic—we speak of the wonders of achievement through discipline, but there's nothing that teaches us so well the value of it as in the harsh resultant experiences of our actions, otherwise called Karma.

Sam

"Watch, Sam. Watch, watch. . ."

Fwuump! A shackled pigeon landed gently on the thick grass a few feet away from where we were standing. Sam gave me a puzzled look and wagged his tail. I signaled for Larry, my assistant who stood a short distance away, to fire the blank pistol. Sam perked up at the sound and looked around.

"I think we've got 'im now, Larry. Fire again and toss another pigeon over here." I took the collar off of the English Pointer and sat him between my legs facing Larry.

"Watch, watch, watch. . ." I said, pointing in Larry's direction.

Bang! Fwuump! Sam stretched out lazily on the grass, turned on his back and pawed the air playfully. I went over to where the pigeon landed, picked it up and showed it to Sam. The dog turned away, uninterested.

Larry walked up to where we were. "Not exactly birdie, is he?"

"That, my friend, is the understatement of the century. I've never seen anything like it! English Pointers are supposed to be the birdiest dogs of all. Even puppies have been known to point anything that moves: beetles, butterflies, songbirds, anything. But this dog. . ." I nodded toward Sam, "has no desire to hunt in the field, and he doesn't care about birds even when they are laid at his feet!"

I thought for a moment. "Maybe *that's* it!"

"Maybe that's what?" Larry asked.

"Maybe he doesn't like pigeons." Larry looked at me skeptically.

"What do you mean? A bird's a bird."

"Wrong! I remember a guy back in Ohio we used to call "Old Swede." He owned a German Shorthaired Pointer named Eric who didn't like pigeons. In our practice trials, Eric would locate the planted pigeon and point it. But every time Old Swede approached to flush it, Eric would break point, walk over and heist (urinate) on the pigeon, then walk away before Old Swede got there. Eric was darned good with pheasants though. That's why I say, maybe Sam doesn't like pigeons. Go get me a couple of pheasants, will you Larry?

Larry took the pigeons back to their hut and released them. He walked over to the pheasant hutch, unhooked the net hanging outside and caught two birds. He shackled their feet and wings, put them in a bag and came back to where I was waiting.

"Okay, fire once and toss a pheasant." Once again Larry shot the pistol in the air and carefully tossed a pheasant toward us. Sam couldn't seem to understand what all the fuss was about. He yawned.

"Give me that other pheasant, Larry." I took the bird, unshackled it, put the bird down on the ground in front of Sam and turned loose my hold. The pheasant froze for a fraction of a second, then keeping low to the ground, it dashed a few feet away before taking flight and disappearing into the far end of the field. Sam regarded the whole scene passively.

"Take the other pheasant back, Larry; I've seen all I need to see." I checked my watch. "His owner will be here pretty soon for his consultation. I'm afraid he's going to be mighty disappointed when he hears what kind of hunting dog he has."

I put the collar and leash on Sam and took him back to the kennel. Sam's indifferent attitude, I learned, extended to dogs as well as birds. As I walked him down the row of runs, he ignored the dogs that sniffed at him and even the ones that barked. I began to formulate the possibilities for Sam's behavior when I heard a car pull into the parking lot.

"Come in, Mr. Rizzo, please have a seat," I said as Sam's owner came in the door. He was a burly man with friendly brown eyes that drooped slightly at the outer corners.

"Well, how did he do?" Mr. Rizzo asked in his Italian accent. I got some bird dog, eh?" He chuckled as if his own question was absurd.

"I'd like to talk with you a little more if I may," I said, sitting down at my desk. The man cheerily nodded his assent.

"Have you spent much time working him? Or running him in the field?"

"Not much. I got to work so I don't have much time to spend with him. My wife, she takes care of him. And the kids, they take him for walks or play with him in the back yard. A wonderful dog with kids," he mused.

"Does he have his own run?"

"Well, he gotta fancy dog house inna back yard, but he likes the house more. The first night we put 'im inna dog house? He howled like

a wolf. So now he stays with us to shut 'im up. He been in ever since."
He chuckled softly to himself. "Yeah, the kids, they just crazy 'bout
Sammy. But when he's trained, the kids just gonna have to find
something else to do on the weekends when I go hunting with him."

"I'm afraid you'd have to hunt alone," I said. "You see, Sam has
absolutely no interest in birds." Mr. Rizzo's face was expressionless,
as if the statement hadn't registered. I continued. "From all physical
appearances, I would say that Sam came from very good breeding.
But, he has none of the hunting instinct that English Pointers are
noted for."

"There's gotta be some mistake!" Mr. Rizzo sputtered. "That
dog cost a lotta money. I buy him to hunt with. Now you tell me he's
not interested in birds?" Mr. Rizzo looked at me incredulously.

"I've checked him out for you, and that's what I've found. Maybe
you'd like to see for yourself." I called Larry to bring a pheasant,
retrieved Sam from his run and went through the same procedure as
before. But this time we tied the pheasant's wings. No sense losing
another one. Afterwards, Mr. Rizzo shook his head sadly.

"I trust you to know your business, Mr. Meisterfeld. It's just that
this was so . . . unexpected. I thought I hadda real good dog. I hadda
lotta plans for him."

"No doubt you did buy a good dog. But it seems that his natural
instincts have been neutralized. The fact that he doesn't relate to dogs
any more than he relates to birds leads me to suspect it's environmental conditioning. In my opinion, he doesn't consider himself a dog
at all." I paused to measure my next words carefully. "You might
consider getting yourself another dog for hunting and let Sam remain
a family pet."

Mr. Rizzo was looking down at the ground, frowning. "No," he
said without moving. "I don't wanna do that. I paid a lotta money for
this dog." He looked up at me. "Can you train him to hunt?"

I thought for a moment. "It's possible that Sam's natural instincts
can be rekindled. But you have to realize that these instincts have
been dormant for . . . how old did you say he is?"

"Twenty months."

"He'll need special training, and lots of it. Equally important is the
fact that his environment and human relationships will have to
undergo a significant change. I'll do whatever is necessary to make a
hunting dog out of him, but it won't mean a thing if he goes back to his
old way of life. Now, I need to know for sure if that is what you want."

Mr. Rizzo looked thoughtful. "That's what I want," he said without hesitation. "My family, they're all outside in the car. Can I bring

them in to say good-bye to Sam?"

I smiled at this request. It was a frequent and familiar one among my clients. In fact, I was about to suggest the same thing myself—but for a different reason. I wanted to see how Sam related to the rest of the family. "Yes, by all means, bring them in."

Mr. Rizzo went outside and returned with his very large wife, who was carrying a small child close to her ample bosom. Mr. Rizzo was holding a little boy's hand.

"Come on in folks, Sam's right here in the office."

As they entered the kennel I was surprised to see four more youngsters in graduating sizes file through the door. When dog and family met it was an uproarious reunion, as if they hadn't seen each other for months rather than hours. Sam became completely unglued as he tried to greet each member of the family at once. In his over-whelming excitement, Sam ended up on his back, sending fountain spurts of urine all over himself. The high-flying emotions that surrounded the scene only confirmed my belief that Sam's problem was environmental.

The first step in Sam's reprogramming was to teach him how to be a dog again. He didn't seem to appreciate the fact that he had a large, inside-outside run all to himself. Or that it was warm and comfortable. I'm sure that as far as he was concerned it was a sad substitute for the high life he'd been accustomed to at home: the soft warm beds at night, the constant attention during the day, the juicy tidbits begged from the dinner table. Kennel living was clearly beneath his dignity and he was quick to protest. He whined, barked and howled right up until dinner-time. I went down the line opening runs, putting the food down and requiring the trained dogs to sit-stay until I gave the okay release command (which is part of their training). When I put Sam's dish down, he took one sniff and walked outside. I guess it didn't smell enough like lasagna.

The sound of metal pans scuttling along the cement floor filled the kennel as each dog licked up the last bits of food clinging to the dish. I went down the row picking up the empty dishes.

"On a hunger strike, eh Sam? I'll check with you before I leave." But his food remained untouched by the time I was ready to go. "Have it your way," I said, picking up the food. I locked up the kennel and crossed the yard to my house. Sam cried and howled for the rest of the night.

The next day was uneventful. I didn't even speak to Sam, but I noticed him watching discreetly as I took other dogs out of their runs and later brought them back. He felt unduly neglected and sulked openly.

At feeding time, Sam again refused to eat. Once more his full dish was picked up. He was quiet that night, but I'm sure his stomach wasn't.

By the third day Sam's resistance began to break down. I guess he decided that *any* human contact was better than none, and that his pride was not worth starving for. That evening when the food was placed in front of him he ate ravenously.

"Well, that's more like it," I said, as I picked up the empty dish. Sam wagged his tail, glad to be noticed. I went to the refrigerator, took out a large juicy bone and returned to Sam's run and offered it to him.

"How about *that*?" I said, grinning. Sam sniffed at it curiously. I suppose after a lifetime of plastic squeak toys and rawhide chewies, he had never known the joys of chewing on a real bone; did not, in fact, even know what to do with it at first. He licked it once, then took it from my hand uncertainly, as if it were hot. He dropped it, sniffed and licked it some, then took it to a corner and began to chew. . .

Sam's opinion of his humble surroundings began to change. He found the kennel, if not luxurious, at least adequate. And even though I was not the catering type, he began to like me. Sam was adjusting.

One day Sam had a visitor. I brought our "Kennel Therapist," Little Orphan Annie, and put her in his run. She was delighted with Sam and pranced up to him to introduce herself. Sam, of course, was wary. He backed up into a corner and sniffed the air cautiously. I watched the two carefully, unsure of how he would react to her. Annie sidled up to him, wagging her tail charmingly. Being stuck in the corner, Sam could only face her. When they were almost nose to nose, she whirled away from him, ran a few steps and spun to face him again. With her head on the ground between her paws, and her rear end up, she barked playfully. I knew that Annie was made for this job. Her skill in thawing out Sam was superb. Intrigued, he approached her. Annie stood very still as Sam sniffed at her timidly. She batted her paw at him lightly. Sam soon forgot his wariness and he and Annie played for hours.

Different dogs were placed in the run next to Sam's off and on for about two weeks. Gradually, Sam felt a bond being formed between him and his own kind. He became curious and bolder toward other dogs; even the ones who barked at him.

All too soon it was time for Sam to begin his obedience training. Here he balked once again. It was work and he was not at all eager to give up his life of leisure. I found it was possible to teach Sam the rudiments of basic obedience, but getting him to like it was something else. In the beginning, it was clearly a test of wills; Sam resisted the training, while I patiently persisted. I knew who would win out in the end. Every day Sam was inevitably worked, and every day a little more resistance dropped away. The more he accepted the training, the more I praised and encouraged his acceptance, and he actually began to like it!

Only after Sam's obedience training was complete and he had mastered the "ho" command (which stops the dog when he is running), was he taken out to the field. With a forty-yard light check cord attached to Sam's collar, I taught him first to range. Normally, English Pointers have a natural instinct to range, but of course Sam was an exception. He learned how to quarter; make left and right turns; respond to whistle and hand signals. I have a method of teaching left and right turns by whistle control only for the purpose of working in high cover where the dog would not be able to see hand signals. Sam learned to "ho" at a distance and come in on a whistle. Eventually, he was freed of the check cord.

When Sam mastered the mechanics of hunting, I had Larry plant birds in the field for him to locate. Larry tied 100-foot-long strings to the wire cages that held the birds in place, so that by pulling the string, I could release the pigeons. After the birds were planted, I'd then take Sam out to the field. I watched him carefully, and when he indicated that he'd gotten the slightest scent of pigeon, I'd release the bird. By not giving him enough time to fully register the scent, Sam was enticed to chase the bird to find out exactly what it was. After a week of "teasing" him this way, I began to delay releasing the pigeons so that Sam gradually came closer and closer before they'd fly away. This method worked so well that Sam tried to catch the pigeons in flight. When his hunting desire strengthened and he became "birdy," I discouraged him from trying to grab the bird, and encouraged him to point instead. Eventually, we switched over to pheasant.

It was a long process from start to finish before Sam was pronounced a bird-dog. He had undergone an amazing transformation from an overindulged, humanized house pet to a graceful, confident hunting dog. It was time for Sam to go home.

"I'd like you to sit downwind here by these bushes so Sam won't see or smell you," I said to Mr. Rizzo. I was preparing to demonstrate Sam's abilities and I needed the dog's full attention. "Try not to make any overt moves or sounds. I don't want him to know you're here yet."

SAM GRADUALLY CAME CLOSER AND CLOSER....

I disappeared behind a row of trees and reappeared moments later with Sam on a leash. "Ho," I said, and Sam stood still. I unsnapped the leash and walked about twenty-five feet away. I stopped and made a wide "follow me" jesture with my arm and gave the hie-on command at the same time. Sam took off instantly, passed me and began to sweep the area in front of me. We worked our way into some high cover where all that could be seen of Sam was the movement of the grass.

I sounded my whistle three times and the movement in the grass changed direction to the right toward a fence line and a row of trees. I sounded my whistle twice more and grass tops moved left. Sam emerged from the high cover then suddenly stopped to sniff the air. He began moving slowly in the direction of the scent. Mr. Rizzo watched, transfixed, as Sam's body tensed and froze in the classical pointing stance before a clump of weeds.

I approached slowly, cautiously, toward the planted pheasant. With my boot I carefully turned the cage over. WHOOSH! Bringing the gun to my shoulder, I aimed and fired; the bird fell about 150 feet away. "Fetch!" I commanded, and Sam shot off in the direction of the bird. Seconds later he was back, sitting in front of me with the handsome cock pheasant in his mouth. "Give," I said, and the dog released the bird into my hand. "Good boy!"

"Sam, Sam!" Mr. Rizzo cried as we approached. "You are wonderful!" Sam greeted him enthusiastically for several minutes, then sat by his side, proud and happy.

"He is a different dog," Mr. Rizzo said, beaming. "How did you get him to like the birds?" he asked.

"I got him to like being a dog," I replied matter of factly. "The rest came naturally." Mr. Rizzo shook his head in wonder.

I was pleased too. Mr. Rizzo had followed my advice on changing the home environment. He had bought guinea pigs for the kids, and built a fenced pen for Sam in the back yard where he stayed when not hunting. But for me there were other dogs to train, other challenges to meet. The memory of Sam's triumph began to fade; that is, until Mr. Rizzo called several months later.

"I'm so happy with my Sammy," he said delightedly. "He is a fine, fine hunter now. In fact, I can hardly get him to quit sometimes!"

I laughed. "Well, Mr. Rizzo," I said. "Sam is like the little boy who loved to go fishing all the time until one day he found out about girls. Sam found out about birds."

Amber

Is it possible for dogs and humans to communicate telepathically? Many times when a dog is left with me for a lengthy stay, the owners are unsure of their exact return date. Yet forty-eight to seventy-two hours before I receive any word that they are back (or on their way back) their dog will let me know ahead of time by anxiously whining and pacing. So when I receive a phone call or a post card from the people, I'm generally not surprised. I've even worked with some dogs that were capable of responding to mental commands. One particular experience has convinced me that it is possible for the mind of a dog to tune in to the mind of its owner, especially when there is a strong devotion and emotional tie. Such was the case of Amber, a cross-bred female, and her owner Barbara Williams.

I had trained a dog for Mr. and Mrs. Williams once before. I liked them both and they seemed like a happy couple. He was a highly successful businessman, and she was an attractive, energetic woman. I hadn't heard from them for many years when one day I got a call from Barbara. She hardly sounded like the same person as she told me about a new dog they had acquired.

"Steve had gotten her about a year ago, after our other dog had died," she said. "Soon after we had gotten Amber, Steve went into a deep depression and wasn't able to find himself again. I tried to help him, but I just couldn't seem to reach him. He took his own life about four months ago."

The abruptness of this news numbed me into silence. I didn't know what to say.

"Amber was with him at the time," she went on. "She was very attached to him, and since then she has become increasingly nervous and high strung. She hates to be left alone and always wants to be with me. She's terrified of strangers too, and is getting overly protective of me." We made arrangements for her to bring the dog up to me.

When Barbara arrived the next day with her dog, she looked pale and haggard. The past four months had been difficult. Amber didn't look any better. Barbara needed time to get beyond her personal grief, and Amber needed to be brought out of hers, so it was decided to leave the dog for therapy and training.

With such a close relationship between Barbara and Amber, I was surprised that the dog was quiet after being left with me. I half-expected her to howl a great deal. But a whole month passed and there wasn't even a whimper from Amber. When I wasn't working her, she spent most of her time curled up in a corner of the inside run, hardly visible in the shadows.

One Monday morning as I was putting a dog through its paces in the training ring, a mournful cry emanated from the other side of the wall where the runs were. It was such an eerie, human-like wail that I froze in my tracks. I hadn't had any new dogs in for the past two weeks, yet I didn't recognize which dog was howling. The sound welled up again and echoed through the kennel. I felt goose bumps rising on the back of my neck.

I walked down the paneled wall looking through the observation peepholes to see if I could discover which dog was making the sound. "Rrrrrrrrwhoooooo!" I listened closely and moved toward the sound. Looking through one of the holes, I saw that it was Amber. I thought it odd that she would wait this long before complaining; such a delayed reaction was highly unusual. I dismissed the matter and returned to training.

Amber continued to wail for another five minutes, then she stopped as abruptly as she had started. I took her out for some training and her responses hadn't altered, so I thought nothing more about it.

The next morning, out of the perceptible quietness of the kennel, I heard Amber's mournful cry again. I checked the clock. It was 10:10, about the same time she'd begun to howl the day before. I listened to see how long she would keep it up. After about eight minutes she was quiet once again.

For the next three mornings I noted the times when Amber's howling took place. It seemed to vary between 10:10 and 10:20 in the morning.

When Saturday came I waited for Amber to repeat the pattern she'd established for the past five days, but the time came and went without her making a sound. In fact, she remained quiet clear through to Tuesday. I called Barbara that afternoon to discuss Amber's behavior.

212

I SAW THAT IT WAS AMBER...

"No, she's never howled before." Barbara answered when I questioned her about it. "Except once," she said.

"When was that?"

"After my husband's death. The neighbors heard her howling for hours before I came home that day."

"I see. Well, she's howled every day, Monday through Friday last week, and around the same time each day. It seemed odd to me because she has never made a sound before or since."

"Yes, that is strange. What time did she howl?"

"In the mornings between 10:10 and 10:20, give or take a couple of minutes." Then without thinking I asked her, "Did anything unusual happen to you around those times last week?"

"No. . ." she said slowly. "I'm on my way to work at that time."

I felt compelled to press on. "Were you thinking or feeling anything unusual?" There was a guarded silence. "Please excuse my questions, Barbara. I don't mean to pry or anything. I'm just trying to understand what made Amber react so strangely. I thought it might have been linked with you somehow, but I guess it's just something that can't really be explained."

"That's all right, Bill," she said softly. "Maybe it did have something to do with me. You see, I have to cross the Bay Bridge every morning about the same time you mentioned. I think last week was the hardest time I've had since Steve died. It seemed like the whole world was on my shoulders. I felt depressed over what had happened and guilty that perhaps I hadn't done everything I could have to help him." She took a deep breath. "Every morning when I crossed that bridge I had the fleeting notion to stop my car and slip quietly over the railing. I didn't, of course, and the feeling left me as soon as I got off the bridge. But it doesn't seem possible that Amber could pick up my mood sixty miles away."

"It may not be possible," I said. "But it's quite a coincidence. How do you feel now?"

"Oh, much better. I went on a small trip over the weekend to relax and rethink some things. By Monday I had no more dreadful thoughts as I crossed the bridge."

"That would explain why Amber has been quiet since Saturday."

We left it at that. I was fairly certain that Amber had tuned into Barbara's thoughts and feelings, but I wasn't sure what Barbara really believed.

Another month went by and Amber was making progress. She was accepting my authority, relating to me better, and enjoying her working sessions more. Barbara called one afternoon to see how Amber was doing. She sounded much improved, and was even able to laugh again.

"Has Amber sung you anymore morning seranades?" she asked jokingly.

"No, she hasn't. But she did howl yesterday afternoon around 2:30." I heard Barbara's breath catch.

"That's really wierd," she said shakily. "I went home early yesterday. I'd been feeling so much better about everything. But as I crossed that bridge coming home, those negative thoughts started to claw at me again, so I mentally dumped *them* over the bridge. I can't tell you what a relief that was! I guess Amber really *did* sense what I was thinking!"

I was glad that Barbara had overcome what must have been a tremendous burden. She contacted me several weeks after Amber went home to report that both her and the dog were doing fine. I'll never forget my experience with Barbara and Amber; it was a perfect example of how some dogs are capable of reflecting our mental and emotional states of being. If they could only talk!

and man was given dominion

over the animal kingdom.